CW00433085

The Era of Uncertainty

Parus,

Never thought the content would be so relevent this quickly!

Enjoy,
Francois

The Era of Uncertainty

GLOBAL INVESTMENT STRATEGIES FOR INFLATION, DEFLATION, AND THE MIDDLE GROUND

François Trahan
Katherine Krantz

WILEY

John Wiley & Sons, Inc.

Published by John Wiley & Sons, Inc., Hoboken, New Jersey.
Published simultaneously in Canada.

For general information on our other products and services or for technical support, please contact our Customer Care Department within the United States at (800) 762-2974, outside the United States at (317) 572-3993, or fax (317) 572-4002.

Wiley also publishes its books in a variety of electronic formats. Some content that appears in print may not be available in electronic books. For more information about Wiley products, visit our web site at www.wiley.com.

Library of Congress Cataloging-in-Publication Data:
Trahan, Francois, 1969–
    The era of uncertainty : global investment strategies for inflation, deflation, and the middle ground / Francois Trahan and Katherine Krantz.
        p. cm.
    Includes index.
    ISBN 978-1-118-02773-8 (hardback); 978-1-118-13407-8 (ebk); 978-1-118-13409-2 (ebk); 978-1-118-13408-5 (ebk)
    1. Investment analysis. 2. Macroeconomics. 3. Uncertainty. 4. Business cycles. I. Krantz, Katherine, 1972– II. Title.
    HG4529.T733   2011
    332.6—dc22
                                                                        2011016570
Printed in the United States of America
10 9 8 7 6 5 4 3 2 1

To Ben Bernanke . . . thanks for the material.

Contents

Foreword

Pick your own cliché: You can't see the forest for the trees; hindsight is 20/20. However you want to phrase it, there is some truth to these statements, particularly when it comes to the broad macro trends that affect financial markets. Macro market trends are sometimes like one of those magic picture posters or an optical illusion with a dual image: It doesn't make sense at first, but as soon as you see the hidden image, it's impossible to un-see it.

Over the past several years, investors have been through many of these "a-ha!" moments as we have witnessed a series of once-in-a-generation economic and market moves. Take a look at what happened during the height of the credit crisis in 2008. During that year, the S&P 500 Index experienced its worst fall since the 1930s, dropping 37 percent. Only 25 of the stocks in that index posted positive performance for the year. Taking a look at the other 475 companies shows that the variance in performance was significant—for example, stocks in the consumer staples sector fell only 15 percent, while those in the financial sector lost more than 55 percent.

For those of us who are professional investors focused on active management, the most important call that could have been made was to predict that risk assets were headed over a cliff. Equity markets took a hard hit, and only the severity of that hit was up for debate. Investors who were focused only on the traditional bottom-up fundamentals that drive stock prices (industry positioning, strength of management, cash flows, etc.) and who were looking for competitive advantages that would help individual stock prices weather the storm no doubt experienced their "a-ha" moment sometime around October 2008—a month in which the S&P 500 Index fell almost 17 percent. At that point, the landscape was certainly not a pretty sight, and it became clear to almost everyone that top-down macro forces were the hidden picture in the image that could no longer be un-seen.

Merely recognizing that top-down forces can overwhelm markets is only half the battle; the more important half is figuring out how to interpret these forces and investing accordingly. The real trick in interpreting and profiting from macro trends lies in decoding the signals sent by the ebb and flow of the business cycle, and few people in the financial industry have done this better than François Trahan.

Over the years, François' insightful analyses of the business cycle have led to market calls that have both benefitted investors on the upside and (more important to many) protected them from losses on the downside. François' incredible track record in successfully interpreting the trends that can be found in leading indicators and other macroeconomic data have also led to his well-deserved reputation as an expert in sector rotation—providing investors positioned on both the long and short sides of the market with opportunities to profit from his ideas. In my opinion, his most important and influential macro prediction to date was his call in the middle of the last decade when he predicted that the worst housing crisis in American history would soon be upon us, and that it would have far-ranging implications for both the global economy and world financial markets.

In 2005, François used his business-cycle-investment framework to shed light on how investment bubbles were both created and destroyed. By definition, it's impossible for the investment public as a whole to know when markets are in the midst of a bubble (otherwise, there wouldn't be bubbles). François' research, however, showed that not only did bubbles exhibit fairly predictable patterns, but more importantly, that markets appeared to be in the stranglehold of a real estate mania at that very time. In retrospect, signs of the real estate bubble could have been obvious to everyone (consider that the phrase "liar loans" was being used in a completely non-ironic context), but they weren't. François' research showed that the real estate market was exhibiting most of the telltale signs of a bubble in its late stages, but at the time, his findings were considered out-of-consensus and somewhat controversial. Even more alarming was his conclusion that the fallout of the bubble bursting could reach much further than just the housing market. Many investors (including his own employer at the time) chose to ignore the implications of his research, and learned an expensive lesson about the macro behavior of markets during a severe downturn. Those who saw the bigger picture and acted accordingly, however, were spared at least some of the pain.

Markets do not need to be in the grip of a mania or in the midst of historic collapse in order for top-down analysis to be important; in the age of increasing globalization, the significance of macro influences even during benign times is likely to increase. The players in the global economy are growing increasingly interdependent, and policy and investment decisions made on one side of the world almost inevitably affect markets on the other. Thanks in part to the growing importance of multinational corporations, the line between developed and emerging economies is becoming more blurred day by day, and technology has hastened the speed at which information travels around the world. Ironically, as the investment world becomes a smaller place, the magnitude of cycles may become larger and larger. This means that getting the big picture right will also become ever more important to investors.

Without a doubt, macro views about the economy and asset class trends play an important role in investment returns. As an active manager of investors' portfolios, I'll be the first to say that company-specific information will always be a critical input for stock pickers, but it is only a portion of the full picture. As François so succinctly summarizes, macro matters.

Robert Doll
Vice Chairman and CIO
of Global Equities,
Blackrock Advisors, LLC

Preface

The recent credit crisis in the United States ushered in a new era of uncertainty. In some ways it was just another bubble in a long line of financial manias. Like any other bubble, it was born out of an extended period of easy money that fueled prosperity, engendered speculation, and ended in a spectacular crash. In some very important ways, however, the lingering impacts are different than the bubbles of recent memory.

This mania was not the same as a euphoric run up and crash of technology stocks; it was an assault on two of the four pillars holding up middle-class America: homes and credit. The other two pillars—employment income and investments—were collateral damage. Even for people who have regained their investment losses and hung onto their jobs, the experience of the last several years has created a generational mistrust of the financial system, in many ways similar to the legacy of the Great Depression. No longer can people count on ample access to credit, increasing home values, and abundant job opportunities to propel them into a better lifestyle than their parents enjoyed. For the first time in decades, the current generation is earning a lower income on average than the one before. This generation feels misled by Wall Street, the government, their mortgage brokers, the credit card companies, and a whole host of other bad guys.

There is a tremendous amount of mainstream books and web sites that cover the credit crisis, but the following chapters will present a different perspective. The book examines the creation and aftermath of bubbles from a top-down perspective, specifically the recent credit/housing bubble, and shows how applying a macro framework could have helped investors better navigate the crisis. The usefulness of the macro framework is not limited to manic periods, however. A business-cycle approach to investing is offered, which can be successfully applied in the various inflationary and deflationary periods anticipated in the next several years. Professional investors, as well as sophisticated individual investors, should find that adding a macro-driven component to their investment process will help to anticipate changing market conditions and to direct the reallocation of their portfolios.

The book begins by examining the influence of macro analysis in the markets. It brings to light how top-down forces influence the direction of financial markets and how including macro analysis in one's research improves the odds of investment success. Importantly, some of the pitfalls of ignoring macro in the investment process are detailed, followed by a review of the role that macro plays in the past, present, and future.

As the chief investment strategist at Bear Stearns, François Trahan had a unique perspective working for one of the major players in the crisis. In the second section, his perspective from the front lines at Bear Stearns is discussed, particularly how a greater focus on macro conditions could have helped the firm successfully navigate the top of the housing bubble.

In the third part of the book, the analysis moves into the present. There is a review of some of the difficult choices that governments and policy makers must make, and where current policies are taking the markets and the economy.

Next the book delves into how to invest for an uncertain future. An exploration of inflation and how it impacts the economy leads into a macro framework for investing during periods of inflationary and deflationary pressures. The view that pricing pressures already in the pipeline will lead to inflation, tightening, a growth slowdown, and possibly disinflation is the base case scenario, but many variations could play out in the years ahead depending on the path of policy. Most importantly, some ways in which to profit from the various macro-driven scenarios are suggested.

Finally, some creative solutions are presented to address the unsustainable path of policy in the United States, as well as implications for the future of the financial services industry.

The dynamic nature of the investment process presented in *Era of Uncertainty* lends itself well to an interactive feature. A companion web site to the book offers readers the ability to input their own current assumptions for inflation and growth and receive a set of macro-driven investment recommendations for each combination. Readers may select between expectations of inflation, deflation, and middle ground for the inflation backdrop; and between boom, bust, and middle ground for the growth environment. Each pairing of inflation and growth expectations yields a broad asset allocation recommendation, such as stocks, bonds, precious metals; a sector allocation suggestion, such as early-cyclical sectors or defensive sectors; and a factor preference for stock selection, for example beta, pricing power, or valuation.

Acknowledgments

From François Trahan:
I would like to thank the members of my strategy team whose research over the years helped to build the framework for this book. Michael Kantrowitz is the best investment strategy mind I have been fortunate enough to work with; he raises the bar on everything I do. Stephen Gregory never fails to remind me that an advanced degree does not teach you to question consensus. Thanks to Joe Ramirez and Emily Needell for help with data, charts, and other background materials. A debt of gratitude also is owed to my wife and children for putting up with my rants on monetary and fiscal policy at home, thank you.

From Katherine Krantz:
An enormous thank you to Tim Klug, Sr., for providing invaluable feedback and editing on first drafts of the chapters; the depth and breadth of his knowledge is astounding. He also offered a fresh perspective and made the final product infinitely better. Brock Moseley, my friend and partner at Miracle Mile Advisors, was incredibly supportive of my participation in this book. The countless hours we have spent discussing how to solve the world's problems have certainly helped hone my views on the markets and beyond. My significant other, Tim Klug (Jr.), lends love and support to everything I do. Thanks for listening and debating with me, and for being my biggest fan (and vice versa). Finally, thanks to my dad for making me watch *Wall $treet Week* with him on Friday nights when I was 10 years old. I miss you.

The Era of Uncertainty

P A R T

I

WHY "MACRO MATTERS"

Macro forces do not influence the decisions of all investors, but they should. The importance of top-down trends to equity returns has ebbed and flowed over the last half century, but increasing globalization has propelled their impact to an all-time high. Although a vast majority of investors indicate that the role of macro in the investment process is greater today than 10 years ago, still more than two-thirds specify bottom-up, fundamental analysis as the most important component.[1] Some bottom-up loyalists are probably incorporating top-down factors into their discipline without realizing it, but many are not and simply leaving money on the table.

There is no dispute that a company's balance sheet and quality of its management team are informative for the relative performance of a stock, but they tell little about the overall backdrop for equities. This is equivalent to knowing that today is going to be warmer than yesterday; unless you also know the season, the relative change in the temperature is not terribly helpful. Accurate information about the health of the overall market environment is particularly important during periods of broad market declines, such as the aftermath of a bubble.

Macro analysis helps the investor move beyond a general buy, sell, or hold decision; it sheds light on the performance dynamics within

1

the market as well. The most powerful way to incorporate macro into the investment process is through a business-cycle approach. Equities exhibit distinctly different behaviors at various points in the economic cycle, and understanding these differences is the key to successful investing. Leading economic indicators provide a very good indication of future economic activity, while stocks themselves are a discounting mechanism for future economic growth. As a result, there is a tight correlation between leading indicators and the equity market. There is no perfect data series to predict stock market movements, but history shows that the movements in leading indicators can serve as a guide to investing successfully across all phases of the business cycle. Macro forces buffet all portfolios; the advantage lies with those investors who harness its power to steer their portfolios versus those who fight against it.

What Is Macro, and Why Should Investors Care?

History doesn't repeat itself, but it does rhyme.[1]

—Mark Twain

People absorb information about macro-economic themes every day without realizing they are doing so. Newspapers and web sites— financial and non-financial alike—are filled with stories about the over-arching macro trends unfolding all over the world. If asked generally, most people would probably say that they know little about macro, but if questioned about the state of the housing market or the influence of China, most would likely come off as fairly well informed. The same goes for investors—the majority claim that they are stock pickers who focus solely on bottom-up company analysis. In reality, they often are choosing these stocks based on bigger-picture trends guiding the entire industry. The influence of macro extends far beyond what most people realize.

Question: If macro is so ubiquitous, then what exactly *is* it?

Answer: It is the force(s) that dictate how the world unfolds around us.

Macro permeates many aspects of day-to-day life. The cult of home ownership in the United States was rooted in political and monetary policies handed down from Washington, D.C. Ultimately, this was embraced by the population at large and fueled the expansion and bursting of the housing bubble. Americans' adjustment to the new reality of less-available credit is reshaping spending patterns and lifestyles. This is just one of many unfolding macro trends that is important to markets. The aging of the enormous Baby Boomer generation is a force that will impact health care in this country for the next 30 years. The emergence of a new consumer class in China will change the balance of trade and economic power around the world. The technology revolution is giving a voice, and power, to people in far corners of the world that were until now largely silent. The accelerating pace of globalization is changing the face of trade, information flow, market movements, and even culture. The analogy of a butterfly flapping its wings felt halfway across the world is truer than ever for global markets.

Ten major macro themes developing today will significantly affect investors' portfolios, both directly and indirectly, in the years to come. These themes are:

1. Globalization
2. The internet and the technology revolution
3. The implications of the credit bubble
4. The rise of China and its emerging consumer class
5. A change in worldwide demographic trends
6. Americans' evolving relationships with credit and debt
7. Fiscal crises in the developed world
8. Troubles for the euro and/or the dollar
9. The Federal Reserve's dual mandate and its shortcomings
10. The changing face of "greed" on Wall Street

The investment implications of several of these market-moving trends are addressed directly in the book, but these forces do not exist in a vacuum. Each of them impacts the analysis in some way. In many cases, the implications of one theme lead directly into another, especially with respect to policy action taken. Take for example the sustained cycle of easy monetary policy following the bursting of the technology bubble in 2000. Federal Reserve Chairman Alan Greenspan lowered interest rates repeatedly as the markets corrected from the heights of the late 1990s. Following the technology meltdown were the 9/11 terrorist attacks and a series of corporate accounting scandals, such as Enron and Tyco, that kept the markets on shaky ground. The solution in each case was lower interest rates. The chart in Figure 1.1 shows the lifecycle of several market themes of the past 20 years and their relationship to the U.S. monetary policy rate.

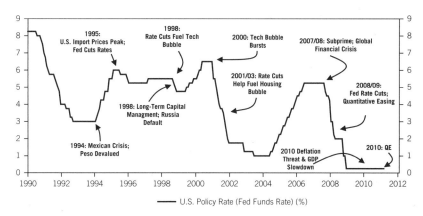

Figure 1.1   Federal Reserve Policy Fuels the Bubble Environment
Source: Wolfe Trahan & Co.

The rock-bottom interest rates that helped pull the economy out of the doldrums after the crises of the early 2000s laid the ground work for a massive expansion of credit. Easy access to credit helped fuel the housing boom of the 2000s, and the subsequent bubble that rocked the latter years of the decade. Although the federal funds rate was increased throughout 2004 and 2005, the damage was done and the economy is still sorting through the rubble. The extremely easy policy that Chairman Greenspan's successor, Ben Bernanke, put in place in the years following the bursting of the credit bubble fueled the massive run-up in commodity prices. Only time will tell what the exact nature of the next bubble will be, but certainly it will come. Without a doubt, macro matters for investors!

Macro Explains More Than 70 Percent of Equity Returns

Ignoring macro is like ignoring the seasons when trying to predict the weather. Any December day in New York City is likely to be a cold one. The "macro" backdrop dictates wearing a coat instead of shorts. The "stock specific" issues determine whether that coat should be a winter parka or a lighter jacket. It's possible to decide incorrectly on the choice of coat, but regardless one is usually better off wearing a coat than shorts in December in New York City.

Macro trends influence everything that happens in the markets, but the extent of its sway is probably a surprise to even those who embrace these trends. Investors who actively harness the powerful influence of macro and use it to their advantage can set themselves apart from the pack.

Investors often have a difficult time explaining the performance of their stock picks. This is largely because they underestimate the influence that macroeconomic forces have on individual stocks. They search for a connection between returns and earnings or management strength, but the truth is that an overwhelming majority of stock performance is explained by forces that go beyond the income and cash flow statements. In fact, the data show that historically 71 percent of equity returns are explained by macro trends.[2] This means that all of the time stock pickers spend poring over balance sheets and talking with company management accounts for less than one-third of a stock's performance. How many investment managers would willingly admit that they are investing blindly with respect to two-thirds of the factors driving their portfolio's return?

One of the prevailing trends over the past several years has been the heightened influence of top-down analysis and a renewed focus on macro. While some stock pickers may have been fortunate

Figure 1.2   Macro Explaining a Record High Percentage of Equity Returns
Source: Wolfe Trahan & Co.

Wolfe Trahan Client Survey

How has the role of macro in your investment process changed in the past 10 years: Increased or Decreased?

Direction	Percentage
Role of Macro Increased	96.3
Role of Macro Decreased	3.7

Survey conducted March 25, 2011.
Total respondents to this question: 676

enough to pick winners that outperformed their benchmark indices, most stocks' relative performance trends were whipsawed by the macro-induced market peaks and troughs. Figure 1.2 shows that since late 2008, the percentage of equity returns explained by macro forces has risen steadily and reached a record high 90 percent by the end of 2010! Getting the "big picture" right has become a necessity for top performance results.

Macro's Role in Bubble-Mania

As shown earlier in Figure 1.1, policy moves meant to prop up the economy in the aftermath of the technology bubble actually laid the groundwork for the next bubble. This pattern is not unique, and in fact has repeated itself many times throughout financial market history. Certainly conditions must be ripe for a particular asset to develop into a bubble, but it takes much more than that. Usually it requires easy monetary policy for the bubble to form, and a policy-tightening cycle for the bubble to burst. The reason for this is that after a series of interest rate increases, the accommodative conditions that set the bubble in motion in the first place have dried up. As that bubble deflates, the central bank steps in again with more liquidity to temper the economic slowdown. This once again sets the stage for the beginning of another speculative mania.

It's hard to imagine in the immediate aftermath of a bubble meltdown that investors would get wrapped up in another would-be mania so soon, and history shows that bubbles do change investors' behavior going forward. The lessons learned in the technology bubble that popped in 2000 still impact the way people invest today. The huge multiples paid by investors in the 1990s have led to a preference for companies with lower valuations. Equity market multiples in general have been in decline since the 2000 peak as the excesses work themselves out. Several years after the housing bubble peak, the residential real estate market is still sluggish. Most people are deleveraging their personal balance sheets and have altered their use of debt, choosing to use debit cards instead of credit cards. Lessons learned even as far back as the Asian currency crisis in the late 1990s are still being played out. Most of the Asian countries that stumbled from excessive debt during that period weathered the latest credit crisis better than most countries because they were less leveraged. The mistakes of the past can have a big impact on market trends going forward.

Yet, history also shows that there have been dozens of bubbles going back at least to the Dutch Tulip Mania in the 1600s. The study of human nature sheds some light on why investors fall for a new bubble each time around. One of the winners of the 2002 Nobel Prize for Economics, Vernon Smith, has attempted to address the study of why markets work the way they do through his research in experimental economics. Mr. Smith and his colleagues have produced significant work centered on laboratory-induced stock market bubbles. In the experiments, Mr. Smith and his team look for patterns that emerge from participants' trading activities and draw conclusions about investors' financial market behavior. During a series of 1988 experiments, his team of researchers made some interesting discoveries about how prior experience affects the severity of bubbles and crashes.[3]

Testing 22 simulated market environments, price bubbles formed and then subsequently crashed on 14 of those occasions. Participants' behavior did differ, however, based on their experience with trading. When inexperienced traders were involved, the price bubbles tended to be much more dramatic. Stock prices rose far above fundamental values, and then crashed back to fundamentals late in the stock's lifetime. As participant experience grew, the results changed. More seasoned traders did not avoid bubbles altogether, but the severity did decline. Mr. Smith and his team concluded that experience was the only way to avoid falling into the bubble trap. The laboratory results showed that by the third go around, market participants recognized their past mistakes, and moved the market toward a more fundamentally grounded pricing structure. While this seems like encouraging news for the elimination of bubbles going forward, real life does not tend to play out exactly in this fashion. New participants are entering the financial markets all the time, introducing inexperienced traders who have not yet learned the lessons of bubbles. Also, the time lag between real-life bubbles weeds out the number of people who can gain enough experience to learn from their previous errors in judgment. Unfortunately, what qualifies as "experience" in the laboratory-created markets takes longer to acquire than the lifespan of the typical Wall Street career. The "good news" is that speculative manias tend to follow a predictable path, and it's possible for astute investors to recognize the patterns. Distinguished and experienced investors such as Jeremy Grantham have built very successful careers on identifying and profiting from these macro patterns.

Bubbles are the natural outgrowth of extremely stimulative policies enacted in the wake of an economic slowdown, and these conditions usually hold regardless of whether the bubble forms in commodities, real estate, or equities; or during the 1600s or the 1900s. The rapid succession of recent bubbles—Asian currencies, technology, and credit and housing—is the byproduct of a series of recessions brought upon by the collapse of the previous speculative mania. Figure 1.3 highlights the short timeline from the creation

---

Technology Bubble
- **August 1998:** Long-Term Capital Management Failure & 75bp Fed Rate Cut
- **Y2K** Investments Further Fuel Money Supply
- **1999 - 2000:** Fed Raises Rates by 175bp
- **March 2000:** Nasdaq Peaks

U.S. Housing Bubble
- **2001: U.S. Recession Begins**
- **Jan 2001 - June 2003: Fed Cuts Rates 11 times from 6.5% to 1%**
- **2002:** Annual home price appreciation of 10% or more in CA, FL and many Northeast states
- **2004:** U.S. homeownership rate peaks at 69.2%
- **2004 - 2006: Fed Raises Rates from 1% to 5.5% in 24 Months**
- **Jan 2005:** S&P/Case-Shiller Home Price Index Peaks at 15.7% YoY
- **2005: U.S. Rent Inflation Begins To Accelerate**
- **2007 - 2009:** Fed Cuts Rates by 500 Basis Points & Creates Lending Facilities For Banks
- **Late 2008:** Global Economy In Recession, Widespread Policy Easing

Figure 1.3 Boom-Bust Timeline of the Previous Decade
Source: Wolfe Trahan & Co.

of the technology bubble through the bursting of the credit bubble less than a decade later. Given the increasing frequency of bubbles in the past several decades, it is more important than ever for investors to understand the macro forces at work.

Ideally, an investor would avoid buying into a market when prices and fundamentals are out of sync, but unfortunately, that is not always an option. Shunning the high-flying technology sector in the mid-1990s would have led an investor to drastically underperform the benchmark as the sector grew to more than 30 percent of the S&P 500 Index by market capitalization. Instead of fleeing a bubble, market participants must have a framework to understand how it developed, its typical life-cycle, and, most importantly, how it will eventually burst.

The pre-bubble environment typically is characterized by an easing of credit conditions and the general availability of easy money. Figure 1.4 shows how money supply typically builds and then begins to contract prior to the peak of an asset bubble. Flush with liquidity, this backdrop sets the stage for economic growth, and eventually speculative excesses.

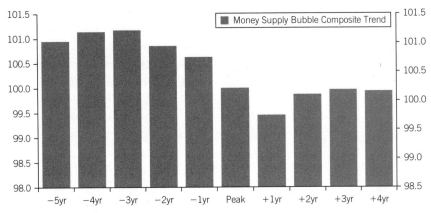

Figure 1.4   Easy Money Sets the Stage for an Asset Bubble
Note: Money Supply = 10 Year Compound Annual Growth Rate, Uses M1 & M2 in 1960s, MZM in 1999/2000
Source: Wolfe Trahan & Co.

At first, the asset-class-specific excesses are not apparent. A booming economy fueled by easy credit causes nearly all asset prices to rise as most of the population enjoys increasing wealth. The birth of the Tulip Mania in 1630s Netherlands was a typical example.

The Dutch Republic was experiencing a Golden Age of high incomes and commercial supremacy, and optimism led to an extremely consumer-oriented nation. At first, the tulip was just a way to brighten the landscape and decorate small gardens, but it quickly became a sought-after status symbol. Tulips had become a sign of wealth and luxury in the country.

The ability to consume and invest more eventually feeds on itself and leads to speculation, as "keeping up with the Jones" becomes a way of life. In the modern economy, house prices are a good proxy for this phenomenon. Homes are typically the largest investment people make, and as everyone now knows, are particularly vulnerable to asset-price inflation. The chart in Figure 1.5 shows how this measure of prosperity increases up until the peak of a bubble.

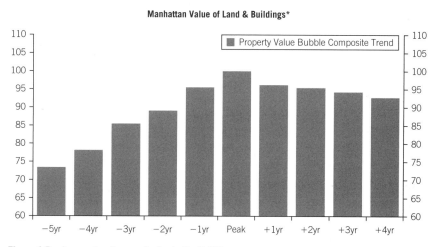

Manhattan Value of Land & Buildings*

Figure 1.5   Increasing Prosperity Fuels the Bubble
Note: Composite = Value of Land and Buildings in Manhattan
Source: Wolfe Trahan & Co.

In Holland, the tulip mania was ripe for speculation since the colors of the flowers were not known until the tulip actually bloomed. Since any bulb could become a *Semper Augustus*, the most valuable strain, trading in these bulbs became highly profitable. As word spread around Europe and attracted more participants, the tulip mania was born.

The euphoria of success causes investors to increase their propensity for risk taking, much as a gambler winning at blackjack

Table 1.1   In 1637, You Could Have Purchased *One* Semper Augustus Tulip Or...

2 Dutch tons of herring	25 guilders
20 gallons of French brandy	30 guilders
2 hogsheads of wine	70 guilders
500 pounds of cheese	60 guilders
1 ton of butter	96 guilders
2 well-fed pigs	60 guilders
Annual earnings of a carpenter	250 guilders
Small town house	300 guilders
1 fat oxen	120 guilders
A ship	500 guilders
24 tons of rye	279 guilders
Typical salary of a middle-ranking merchant	1500 guilders
Typical salary of a well-off merchant	3000 guilders
Highest reliably attested price paid for a tulip bulb (1637)	6290 guilders

Source: Edward Chancellor, *Devil Take the Hindmost,* p.18; Peter M. Garber, *Famous First Bubbles,* p. 82.; Mike Dash, *Tulipomania,* pg. 159

may up his bets with every hand. The media begins to chime in with talk of a "new paradigm," and investing in the asset du jour becomes cocktail party fodder. In Holland, the popular frenzy launched a futures market for tulips. The average Dutch person who was unable to participate in the stock market of the day was able to wager on tulip bulbs, leading to an escalation of the mania. This social reinforcement builds a false sense of security and creates a feedback loop sending asset prices spiraling upward well beyond intrinsic value.

At this point pricing pressures accelerate, typically beginning with raw materials such as commodities. Several years into the tulip bubble, the value of some bulbs would nearly double in little more than a week. Capital rushed into the market and amateur "investors" ponied up all that they had. Volume reached all-time highs with bulbs changing hands up to 10 times per day.

In time, higher prices begin to filter through the greater economy as wage pressures accelerate and lead to higher overall inflation. This forces central bankers to intervene in order to maintain price stability. Eventually the removal of cheap capital squashes speculation.

The tulip mania ended with an internal "liquidity" crisis. Spring was fast approaching, and thus the impending delivery of the bulbs, so rumors began to spread that there were no more buyers. Tulips became unsellable and a spiral of defaults occurred.

The United States Federal Reserve's attempt to control an overheating economy usually goes to extremes in the modern day as well. Not only do policy makers create enough economic drag to break the back of speculative excesses, but almost every Fed tightening cycle has concluded with an economic crisis. Figure 1.6 highlights how changes in the federal funds target rate often trigger the end of a bubble.

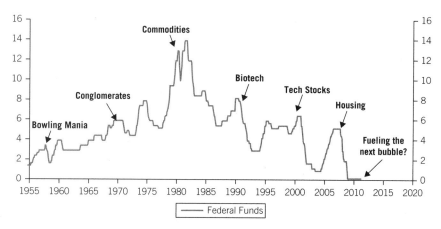

Figure 1.6   Tightening Monetary Policy Marks the Beginning of the End of an Asset Bubble
Source: Wolfe Trahan & Co.

As borrowing costs increase, the economy slows and investors re-price risk. This generally leads to investors abandoning the inflated asset classes, causing prices to fall dramatically. The feed-back loop that elevated prices to such lofty levels operates on the downside as well. In most cases, stock prices and earnings growth have already begun their declines by the time the recession officially begins. In fact, Figure 1.7 shows that stocks have peaked on average about nine months before the start of a major slowdown, earning their status as a leading indicator of the economy.

The post-bubble environment generally depends on how deeply the bubble has penetrated the economy. Thematic bubbles, which

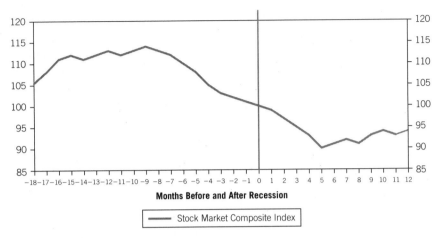

Months Before and After Recession

Stock Market Composite Index

Figure 1.7   Stocks Usually Peak About Nine Months Before the Slowdown Hits the Rest of the Economy

Note: Stock Market Composite derived from railroad stock prices during speculative periods around 1857, 1873, 1884, 1893, 1907, and 1929, and the S&P 500 Index in the late 1960s/ early 1970s and late 1990s/early 2000s periods.

Source: Wolfe Trahan & Co.

occur when a particular asset theme becomes popular and crowd mentality promotes ownership of the group, do not usually leave a massive mark on the economy. The thematic popularity of bowling stocks in the 1960s was just a blip. The "Tulip Mania" became "Tulip Phobia", causing most of the common varieties to never recover their values, but no general economic crisis ensued. Life-changing bubbles, which are often based on new and transformative technologies or infrastructures that change the face of the business world like the internet or railroads, tend to be farther reaching, and have historically led to massive over investment and subsequent economic declines. In the aftermath, with the economy in the throes of recession and anemic growth, policy makers typically begin increasing liquidity to jump start credit creation. This reigniting of credit is typically the link that ties serial bubbles together.

Chapter Summary

- Data show that historically 71 percent of equity returns are explained by macro trends. This means that all of the time stock pickers spend poring over balance sheets and talking with company management accounts for less than one-third of a stock's performance.

- Given the increasing frequency of bubbles in the past several decades, it is more than important than ever for investors to understand the macro forces at work.
- Speculative manias tend to follow a predictable path and it's possible for astute investors to recognize the patterns.
- The pre-bubble environment typically is characterized by an easing of credit conditions and the general availability of easy money. The ability to consume and invest more eventually leads to speculation. Pricing pressures accelerate, central bankers tighten policy to maintain price stability, and the bubble bursts.
- Policy moves meant to prop up the economy in the aftermath of a bubble usually lay the groundwork for the next bubble. Policy moves to end the bubble usually go to extremes, and almost every Fed tightening cycle has concluded with an economic crisis.
- Only time will tell what the exact nature of the next bubble will be, but certainly it will come. Without a doubt, macro matters for investors!

C H A P T E R

The Ever-Changing Macro Landscape

Globalization is a fact of life. But I believe we have underestimated its fragility.[1]

—Kofi Annan

Despite the clear influences of macro on the markets in recent years, most of Wall Street remains very bottom-up focused. Luckily, or perhaps unluckily for that group, they are in for some continuing education as the world persists in becoming a smaller place. *The single biggest macro trend of the past decade has been globalization.* Globalization has been a buzzword in the markets for some time, but the impacts of technological innovation and an interconnected global economy are now vividly on display. Major developments such as the introduction of the Euro and the rise of China have greatly influenced the way the world looks today. Figure 2.1 lists some of the most influential events that have accelerated globalization, dating back to the colonization of the United States from Europe in the late-1400s.

Macro in the Age of Globalization

The correlation among the Gross Domestic Product (GDP) of major economic players is as high as it has ever been, putting macro trends on center stage. Two of the major tailwinds behind this shift are the huge increase in cross-border trade in the last few decades, and the near-synchronization of monetary policy over the last several years. The multitude of free-trade agreements put

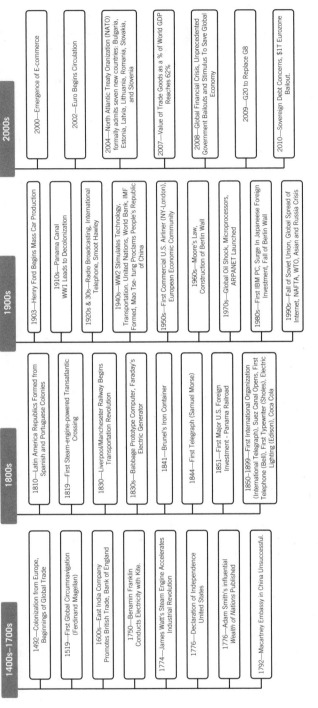

1400s–1700s	1800s	1900s	2000s
1492—Colonization from Europe, Beginnings of Global Trade	1810—Latin America Republics Formed from Spanish and Portuguese Colonies	1903—Henry Ford Begins Mass Car Production	2000—Emergence of E-commerce
1519—First Global Circumnavigation (Ferdinand Magellan)	1819—First Steam-engine-powered Transatlantic Crossing	1910s—Panama Canal WW1 Leads to Decolonization	2002—Euro Begins Circulation
1600s—East India Company Promotes British Trade, Bank of England	1830—Liverpool/Mancheseter Railway Begins Transportation Revolution	1920s & 30s—Radio Broadcasting, International Telephone, Smoot Hawley	2004—North Atlantic Treaty Oranization (NATO) formally admits seven new countries: Bulgaria, Estonia, Latvia, Lithuania, Romania, Slovakia, and Slovenia
1750—Benamin Franklin Conducts Electricity with Kite.	1830s—Babbage Prototype Computer, Faraday's Electric Generator	1940s—WW2 Stimulates Technology, Transportation. United Nations, World Bank, IMF Formed, Mao Tse- tung Proclaims People's Republic of China	2007—Value of Trade Goods as a % of World GDP Reaches 62%
1774—James Watt's Steam Engine Accelerates Industrial Revolution	1841—Brunel's Iron Container	1950s—First Commercial U.S. Airliner (NY-London), European Economic Community	2008—Global Financial Crisis, Unprecedented Government Bailouts and Stimulus To Save Global Economy
1776—Declaration of Independence United States	1844—First Telegraph (Samuel Morse)	1960s—Moore's Law, Construction of Berlin Wall	2009—G20 to Replace G8
1776—Adam Smith's influential Wealth of Nations Published	1851—First Major U.S. Foreign Investment - Panama Railroad	1970s—Global Oil Shock, Microprocessors, ARPANET Launched	2010—Sovereign Debt Concerns, $1T Eurozone Bailout.
1792—Macartney Embassy in China Unsuccessful.	1850–1899—First International Organization (International Telegraph), Suez Canal Opens, First Telephone (Bell), First Typewriter (Sholes), Electric Lighting (Edison), Coca Cola	1980s—First IBM PC, Surge In Japaneese Foreign Investment, Fall of Berlin Wall	
		1990s—Fall of Soviet Union, Global Spread of Internet, NAFTA, WTO, Asian and Russia Crisis	

Figure 2.1 Globalization Has Been in the Making for Hundreds of Years

Source: Wolfe Trahan & Co.

Wolfe Trahan Client Survey

What type of analysis do you use the most in your investment process?

Type of Analysis	Percentage
Bottom-Up Analysis	68.5
Top-Down Analysis	21.3
Quantitative Analysis	8.2
Technical Analysis	2.0

Survey conducted March 25, 2011.
Total respondents to this question: 709

into place during the 1990s sharply increased the co-movement of global economies, and by default, their equity markets. Europe's adoption of the single Euro currency also pushed a significant portion of the global economy further in sync. The chart in Figure 2.2 illustrates the rolling 10-year correlations of several of the world's largest economies with global GDP. During the 1990s, correlations were mixed, and ranged from strongly positive to strongly negative. By the early 2000s, economic activity was clearly more synchronized. As countries increasingly rely on each other to buy the goods they produce, it makes it almost impossible for a major economic crisis in one region not to filter into the rest of the world.

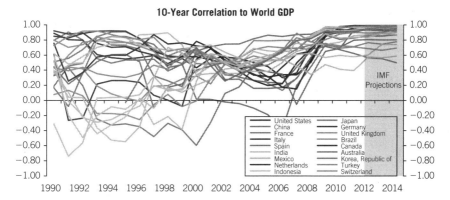

Figure 2.2   GDP Growth Around the World Is Now Highly Correlated
Source: Wolfe Trahan & Co.

In this context, it is no surprise that turmoil such as the European debt crisis had an impact on equities in the United States in 2010. Some suggested that the fragile U.S. recovery would be unfazed by the sovereign crisis spreading through Europe, but this was wishful thinking. Even Treasury Secretary Timothy Geithner suggested at one point that the European turmoil would not hurt U.S. growth.[2] The United States and Europe have the largest bilateral trade relationship in the world, and the two regions together account for more than 50 percent of global GDP. It was only a matter of time before the ripple effects of Europe's debt crisis landed on our shores. The cracks in the plaster appeared in Asian equity markets first as the starting point of the global supply chain, but weakness finally showed up in the S&P 500 in April 2010. The chart in Figure 2.3 illustrates how the equity market in the United States reacted to the crisis in Europe. As the cost of insuring against the risk of default for Spanish debt spiked in the second quarter of 2010, the S&P 500 index began its descent from the April peak.

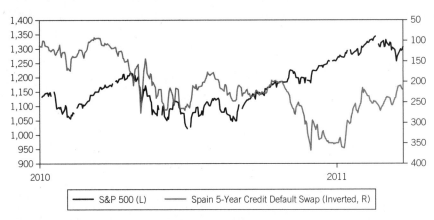

Figure 2.3   As the Cost of Insuring Spanish Debt Against Default Rises, the S&P 500 Takes a Hit
Source: Wolfe Trahan & Co.

The initial jolt from the crisis spreading through Europe is not the end of the story. Ongoing austerity measures put in place to tame the deficits will dampen growth well beyond Europe. The European Union is China's largest trading partner. If the largest export market for the world's engine of growth is hobbled, global growth could be diminished for some time to come.

The crisis also has put downward pressure on the Euro relative to the U.S. dollar. Historically, a stronger dollar would not have been a major concern for the U.S. equity outlook, but in the current policy environment it is bad news. The role of the dollar has transitioned to policy lever with the fed funds rate at zero and fiscal policy options limited. The currency is now the "policy tool of last resort" for the Federal Reserve to stimulate growth, increasing the United States' vulnerability to government policies around the world. The relationship between stocks and the dollar is shown in Figure 2.4. The two series have become strongly negatively correlated—a weaker dollar means higher stock prices, and vice versa. The problems in Europe come home to roost in global equity markets.

Figure 2.4   The Dollar Has Become the Policy Tool of Last Resort
Source: Wolfe Trahan & Co.

The heightened role of the dollar as a policy tool amplifies the economic impact of moves in the currency. The dollar has normally been a safe haven destination for capital during times of crisis, but the Federal Reserve's program of quantitative easing (QE) is beginning to erode the currency's reserve status. QE involves buying Treasury securities to inject liquidity into the markets and drive down interest rates, but it can also raise expectations of future inflation. Higher inflation normally puts downward pressure on a currency since rising prices diminish its value. At the same time, other central banks are actually raising rates to help curb inflation and tame growth. Currencies in countries with higher yields will attract more capital at the expense of low-yielding dollar investments. The official stance of the Federal Reserve was that QE—or "additional purchases of longer-term securities," as Chairman Bernanke referred to it at his infamous speech in Jackson Hole in August 2010—was one of the remaining strategies available to provide additional stimulus.[3] In practice, it meant lifting the economy via the wealth effect of a rising equity market, and depressing the dollar to kick-start the U.S. export sector. An unintended consequence of a weaker dollar, however, is reduced purchasing power for Americans as well as higher commodity prices, further cutting into disposable income. Meanwhile, the powerful Chinese economy could derail what the Federal Reserve is attempting to do by running either too hot (introducing excess inflation by boosting commodity prices even higher) or too cold (failing to act as an engine of global growth).

It is clear that no country is an island with globalization in full effect. Trade, technology, and policy have integrated world economies to the degree that macro forces can and do trump company-specific stories much of the time. The future likely holds more of the same, and to an even greater degree.

The Increasing Role of Macro in the Years Ahead

Over the past 30 years, the pace of globalization has accelerated at an extreme rate and all signs point to this trend continuing in the decades ahead. It is highly likely that a great shift in the balance of economic power will occur as well. According to the International Monetary Fund, so-called "emerging" economies will be as large as advanced economies in terms of GDP by 2013. The convergence of advanced and emerging economies' GDP is shown in Figure 2.5. This means that what takes place in countries like China and India will have a much larger influence on global growth, and the United States, than ever before.

Already, the influential ebb and flow of China's economy is visible in global markets. The world counts on China to sustain a "Goldilocks economy"—neither too hot nor too cold—a term once reserved for the United States in the 1990s. Now the ideal scenario is enough growth in Asia to sustain and stimulate manufacturing in other global economic powers, but not so much demand that commodity prices rise out of control, spark inflation, and induce the People's Bank of China to hit the brakes on monetary policy to tame growth.

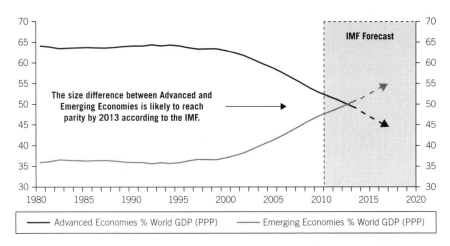

Figure 2.5   Emerging Economies Set to Make Up a Larger Portion of World GDP by 2013?
Source: Wolfe Trahan & Co.

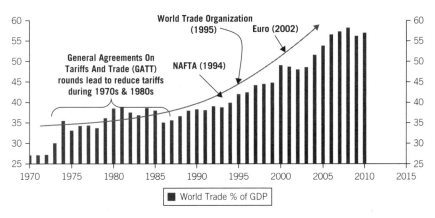

Figure 2.6   Trade Now Equates to More Than Half of World GDP
Source: Wolfe Trahan & Co.

Increased interconnectedness will introduce a new set of challenges in the years to come. Figure 2.6 shows that over the past 40 years, world trade has risen from about 25 percent of GDP to more than half today.

This increase in trade has placed greater importance on managing the global supply of goods, and better methodologies have evolved. Technological innovations in the twentieth century have allowed companies to operate more efficiently through the practice

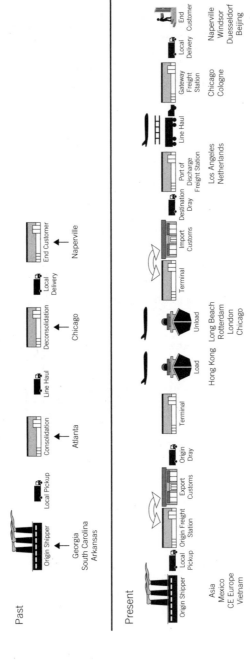

Figure 2.7 The Changing Nature of the Supply Chain—The UPS Example
Source: UPS 2009 Annual Report

of just-in-time inventory management. Companies such as UPS have been integral to this process, helping to optimize the global supply chain. The diagram in Figure 2.7 is an interesting look at how UPS's business has adapted to today's global economy and improved global supply chains.

The Changing Nature of the Supply Chain

The adaptation of just-in-time inventory management has greatly reduced inventory swings that have historically plagued the United States economy during a downturn. Moreover, it has allowed companies to operate more efficiently and profitably by carrying lighter levels of inventory, thus tying up less capital. Figure 2.8 shows the multi-decade downward trend in inventories relative to sales. Lower readings for the inventory-to-sales ratio in the United States were traditionally a sign of economic strength, but today it is also a reflection of companies holding much less inventory.

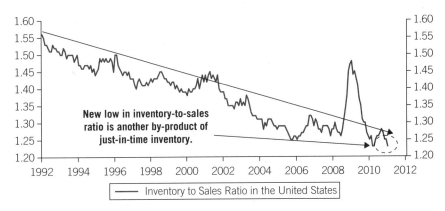

Figure 2.8   Wholesaler's Inventory Continues to Head Lower Relative to Sales
Source: Wolfe Trahan & Co.

One of the foundations of globalization is the supply chain that ships goods all over the world—trade routes are the grease that keeps globalization humming. Any kinks along the way have the potential to disrupt economic activity globally, especially under a just-in-time inventory management system. An example of this occurred when a labor dispute among workers in America's West Coast ports, the world's third largest harbor complex, caused a one-month halt in activity that rivaled the drop in trade experienced in late 2008 during the recession. Figure 2.9 illustrates the export decline that occurred as goods manufactured in Asia were stuck floating on ships for more than a week.

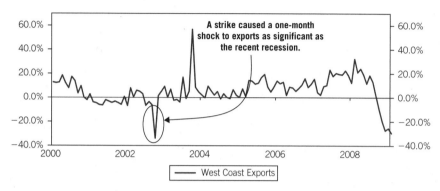

Figure 2.9   Supply Chain Is More Susceptible to Geopolitical Risks
Source: Wolfe Trahan & Co.

The hunt for lower manufacturing costs has stretched the supply chain to all corners of the earth. While the benefits to the global economy have been measureable, the risk associated with manufacturing goods overseas has required a higher level of oversight. In 2007, Mattel had to recall almost 1 million products that were manufactured by a contractor in China because they were covered in lead paint. As companies in several industries have learned, quality and safety standards in emerging countries are not up to the same level that they are in the United States. Similar issues have occurred over the past several years with products ranging from dog food to baby formula. The following text acknowledging the global risks to their business model was included in Mattel's 2009 10-K:

> Mattel's principal manufacturing facilities are located in China, Indonesia, Thailand, Malaysia, and Mexico. To help avoid disruption of its product supply due to political instability, civil unrest, economic instability, changes in government policies, and other risks, Mattel produces its products in multiple facilities in multiple countries.

The impact of globalization is directly reflected in the performance of global equity markets, not just the correlation of GDP. Because a company in the United States might derive a significant portion of its revenues abroad, it is not only affected by the domestic economy, but also by the economies of other counties across the world. Because of this, investors are now forced to acknowledge global economic trends more and more as the inter-connectedness of foreign and domestic company revenues has been on the rise. The chart in Figure 2.10 shows the extent to which equity markets across the world have become correlated over the past 15 years. The data in this chart show that trying to diversify a portfolio just by picking geographical regions has become impossible.

Not only have correlations with the world equity index increased over time, but cross-country correlations have jumped as well. The table in Figure 2.11 shows the correlations for several countries' equity indices as of 1995 and 2010. Clearly, there has been a momentous rise in the unification of global equity markets. A significant fact is that some countries that were negatively correlated in 1995 were significantly positively correlated 15 years later.

The increase in trade also means that corporations derive more and more of their revenues from abroad. This has been a major driver

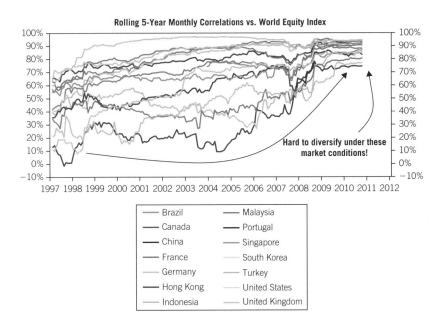

Figure 2.10   Correlations between Equity Markets and World Equities Have Become Extremely Elevated

Source: Wolfe Trahan & Co.

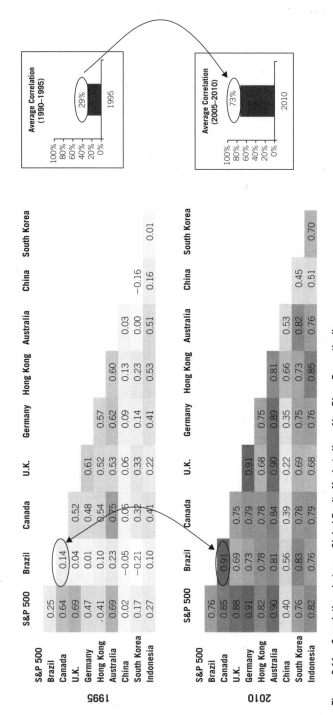

Figure 2.11   Correlations between Global Equity Markets Have Also Risen Dramatically
Source: Wolfe Trahan & Co.

28

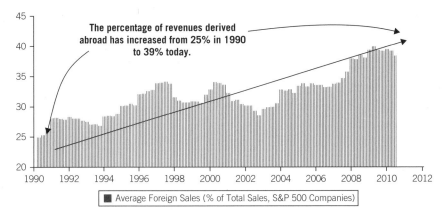

Figure 2.12   S&P Companies Derive Almost 40 percent of Revenues from Abroad
Source: Wolfe Trahan & Co.

of the rise in correlations between country equity indices. Changes in the Chinese economy, for example, are now propagated across the world through increased international trade. The chart in Figure 2.12 shows how the percentage of sales derived abroad has risen fairly steadily over the past decade, a trend that is also seen across the world.

There have been periods when macro trends exerted a lighter force on the markets than normal, but those days have passed. The high correlations across economies and markets are here to stay, and, if anything, should intensify. The increasingly global economic future will keep macro in the spotlight.

Learning from Macro-Driven Markets of the Past

There are phases when top-down trends clearly dominate the market landscape. The last several years of the 2000s—the culmination and aftermath of the housing/credit bubble—were without a doubt part of one of those phases. During this time, the heightened influence of macro manifested itself as a spike in the co-movements of asset classes. Stock pickers became frustrated as compelling bottom-up stories of cash-flush companies and superior market share were trumped by things like trends in consumer spending and currency swings. This period of macro domination has lasted

Table 2.1   Asset Class Correlations Have Risen Markedly

Correlation with S&P 500 Index	1990 to 1999	2008 to 2010	Difference
U.S. Large-Cap Equity	1	1	0
U.S. Small-Cap Equity	0.78	0.95	+0.17
International Equity	0.54	0.93	+0.39
Emerging-Markets Equity	0.57	0.87	+0.31
Real Estate Investment Trusts	0.45	0.83	+0.38
Real Assets	0.08	0.58	+0.51

Source: Standard & Poor's, Russell, MSCI Barra, Nareit, DJUBS

for some time, and in fact, all-time-high readings of correlations across asset classes, countries, and sectors were still climbing throughout early 2011.

Table 2.1 shows the correlation between the U.S. large-cap S&P 500 Index and several other equity benchmarks including U.S. small-cap equities (Russell 2000 Index), international developed-market equities (MSCI EAFE Index), REITs (NAREIT Equity Index), and real assets (DJUBS Commodity Spot Price Index) over two time periods. The period from 1990 to 1999 exhibited almost no correlation between real assets and United States large-cap equities, providing an excellent diversification opportunity. Real Estate Investment Trusts (REITs), emerging-market equities, and even developed-international equities all had positive but still fairly low correlations to the United States. Clearly there were asset class- and region-specific forces at play in addition to the macro backdrop. Not unexpectedly, U.S. small-cap equities had the highest correlation to large caps at 78 percent, but still low enough to provide some meaningful portfolio diversification.

Turning to the period from 2008 to 2010, the data tell a completely different story. During these years, both a devastating correction across most asset classes and a nearly vertical recovery took place. Monetary policy rates were held near zero and the dollar became not only a policy tool, but an asset class unto itself. The correlation between U.S. equities and real assets jumped from 8 percent to 58 percent, as swings in the dollar influenced directional movements in both of these asset classes. The correlation with REITs nearly doubled as the housing market took center stage on the economic landscape. Both developed international and emerging market correlations hovered near 90 percent, providing little refuge as equity markets swung nearly in tandem, and fears of contagion from European fiscal problems permeated the globe. The correlation of small-cap U.S. equities shot up to 95 percent.

Even within the U.S. equity market there was little performance differentiation during this period. Although regularly there are episodes of extremely high correlations across the sectors of the U.S. equity market, as shown in Figure 2.13, the last several years have been an extreme, with average sector correlations reaching more than 90 percent. Despite beginning 2007 with extremely low correlations, there was a spike shortly thereafter as subprime lenders began collapsing and concerns about Freddie Mac and Fannie Mae resurfaced. The financial industry was at the forefront of the crisis, which as a result called the health of the financial markets into question. Equities began their long and nearly indiscriminate retreat. In the following year, there were only 25 stocks in the S&P 500 index that finished in positive territory. The majority of these stocks were in the consumer staples or health care sectors— defensive sectors that tend to perform better in the contraction phases of the business cycle. Not every financial stock in the S&P 500 index deserved the beating it took in the meltdown, but selling was not based on bottom-up fundamentals. "Shoot first and ask questions

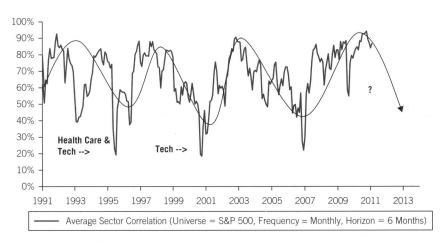

Figure 2.13   Sector Correlations Increased Throughout the Aftermath of the Bubble
Source: Wolfe Trahan & Co.

later" was the only investment strategy to be found in 2008. The rebound in equities following the March 2009 bottom was the mirror image of the retreat. The hardest hit stocks bounced the highest as pro-cyclical sectors led the government stimulus-induced rally into a new expansionary phase of the cycle.

The influence of macro trends is not limited to equities. The convergence of bond yields in the Eurozone prior to the introduction of the Euro was another example of top down triumphing over bottom up. The approaching launch of the single European currency ushered in a period of sinking risk premiums for less economically sound countries, such as Greece and Italy. The markets began pricing these bonds similarly to those issued by stronger Euro-zone countries like Germany. Country-specific default risks and liquidity differentials were disregarded for a period of time as interest rates converged to a lower, pan-Euro-zone level. This macro trend was overwhelmed when the fiscal crisis in Europe helped to expose country-specific risks. Figure 2.14 highlights how bond yields converged in the late 1990s but then finally diverged in the late 2000s.

In contrast to the last several years, there also are periods when the influence of macro forces is less obvious, and highly misunderstood. The height of the technology bubble in 1999 was one of these times. Most people remember this period as the bull market of a lifetime, but in reality only the technology sector, which accounted for 30 percent of the S&P 500 index, was soaring. Figure 2.15 presents the huge differential in returns for the technology sector versus the others in 1999. The broad index itself was up less than a third of the technology sector, and defensive sectors like consumer staples and utilities were even in negative territory for the year.

After the technology market peaked in March, the equity market in 2000 played out almost exactly opposite of 1999—there were pockets of strength despite the overwhelming impression that there was a broad-based bear market. This was not the case. In fact, several sectors posted significant gains in 2000. The graph in Figure 2.16 shows that from the top of the technology bubble in March 2000 through the end of the year, the technology sector fell by roughly 50 percent but industrials, energy, financials, utilities, and consumer staples all ended the year significantly higher. Technology had become the largest sector in the index as the bubble inflated, and as a result it dragged the entire S&P 500 Index down with it as it

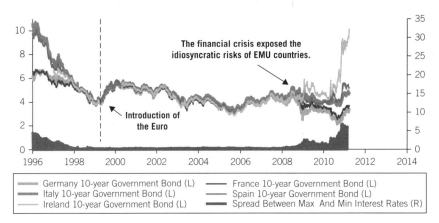

Figure 2.14   Macro Forces Helped European Bond Yields Converge, Until the Latest Crisis Exposed Country-Specific Risks
Source: Wolfe Trahan & Co.

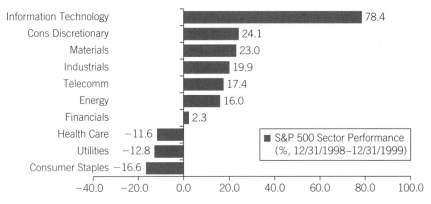

Figure 2.15   The 1999 "Bull Market" Was Largely Confined to a Few Sectors
Source: Bloomberg

fell. Investors who understood the composition of the index, and knew to take shelter in counter-cyclical sectors, made money.

Chapter Summary

- Despite the clear influences of macro on the markets in recent years, most of Wall Street remains very bottom up focused.
- The single biggest macro trend of the past decade has been globalization. The correlation among the Gross Domestic

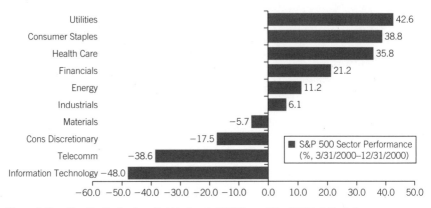

Figure 2.16   After the Technology Bubble Burst, 2000 Was a "Stealth" Bull Market
Source: Bloomberg

Product of major economic players is as high as it has ever been, putting macro trends on center stage. The impact of globalization is also directly reflected in the performance of global equity markets.

- The United States dollar is the "policy tool of last resort" for the Federal Reserve to stimulate growth with interest rates hovering at zero percent. The dollar's new role increases the United States' vulnerability to government policies around the world.
- Quantitative easing depressed the dollar with the unintended consequence of reduced purchasing power for Americans as well as higher commodity prices, further cutting into disposable income.
- There have been periods when macro trends exerted a lighter force on the markets than normal, but those days have passed. The high correlations across economies and markets are here to stay and, if anything, should intensify. The increasingly global economic future will keep macro in the spotlight.

3

Harnessing the Power of the Business Cycle in Investing

We have for the first time an economy based on a key resource [information] that is not only renewable, but self-generating. Running out of it is not a problem, but drowning in it is.[1]

—John Naisbitt

The cornerstone of a successful investment philosophy is the belief that leading economic indicators (LEIs) tend to be very good predictors of future economic activity. The tight relationship between the Institute for Supply Management (ISM) Manufacturing Index, a reliable leading indicator, and real GDP growth in the United States is apparent in Figure 3.1.

Combine with this the notion that stocks typically discount economic growth about six months in advance, and it is easy to see how equity markets are tightly correlated with leading economic indicators. Figure 3.2 shows that over the past 50 years annual price changes in the S&P 500 Index have closely tracked changes in the business cycle.

There is no holy grail of data series that perfectly explain stock returns, but leading indicators' strong historical correlation to equity markets make them worth monitoring. The table in Figure 3.3 shows how the correlation between leading indicators and stock returns has changed over the past five decades. While the relationship waned in the 1980s and 1990s as massive

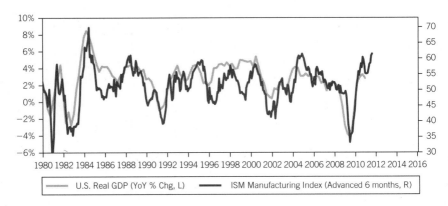

Figure 3.1   Leading Indicators Are Good Predictors of Future Economic Activity
Source: Wolfe Trahan & Co.

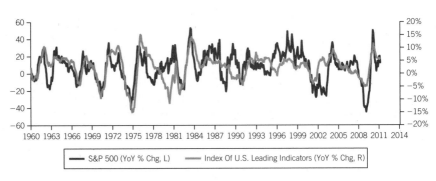

Figure 3.2   Annual Equity Returns Closely Track Changes in the Business Cycle
Source: Wolfe Trahan & Co.

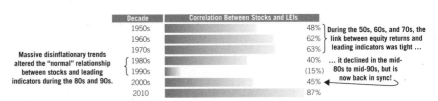

Figure 3.3   The Predictive Power of LEIs Is Currently High
Source: Wolfe Trahan & Co.

disinflationary trends altered these historical relationships, they now seem to be back in sync. The predictive power of LEIs has soared once again.

Macro Is the Bedrock of Successful Investing

Understanding the role of macro is more than just an academic exercise—it is the bedrock of successful investing. Managers who ignore such an important input are leaving money on the table. There is an enormous difference, however, between recognizing the importance of macro and learning how to interpret the stream of data to make better investment decisions. In our experience, the strong relationship between leading economic indicators and stock price movements make them some of the most important indicators to track. It is no surprise that stocks and LEIs exhibit a tight correlation. LEIs are data series that tend to anticipate changes in economic activity several months in advance. Stocks tend to price in trends in economic growth about six month before they occur, making stocks themselves leading indicators.

There are many different types of data series that add value as leading indicators. Each of them measures a different aspect or region of the economy, but most times they tend to move in unison, as seen in Figure 3.4.

Figure 3.4   Most Leading Indicators Are Highly Correlated
Source: Wolfe Trahan & Co.

There are LEIs with shorter lead times, such as regional surveys like the Empire Manufacturing Survey and Philly Fed index, ISM New Orders/Inventories ratio, positive earnings estimate revisions, and the proprietary Wolfe Trahan Leading Economic Index. Intermediate-term indicators are mostly gauges of future inflation, and include consumer prices, commodity prices, and emerging Asia equity markets. There are also several indicators with longer lead times—mostly proxies of monetary policy—such as changes in global short interest rates, money supply growth, the real federal funds rate, and the yield curve. No single series is perfectly predictive, but examined together a trend usually emerges. Keep in mind that forecasting economic growth is not an end unto itself for investors. The ultimate goal is to determine the stage of the economic cycle, and to position a portfolio to profit from the unfolding trends.

A solid understanding of the business cycle is crucial to benefit from the risk-reward shift as leading indicators peak or trough. The characteristics of a portfolio that outperform during a period of deceleration in leading indicators are much different than those of a portfolio that outperforms as LEIs are accelerating.

Figure 3.5 presents a simple business cycle framework corresponding to the peaks and troughs in leading indicators. The framework divides the cycle into four primary stages relating to market expansion and contraction. As LEIs bottom, the economy moves into the

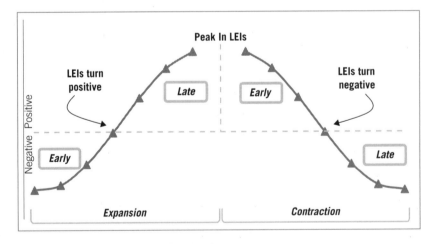

Figure 3.5   A Simple Business Cycle Framework
Source: Wolfe Trahan & Co.

early expansion phase. This is when prospects for future economic growth begin to improve and investors start pricing in better expectations. Based on historical market data, equities tend to post the best returns in this phase of the cycle. Data from 1950 to 2009 indicate that the annualized equity return in this phase is 34.5 percent. During this period, classic early-cyclical sectors such as consumer discretionary (for example, retailers) tend to outperform the broader market.

Once LEIs reach positive territory, the cycle enters its *late expansion*, and equities' average performance is a more subdued 15.8 percent per year, as shown in Figure 3.6. In this period, hyper-cyclical sectors like technology tend to overtake early cyclicals as performance leaders. As leading indicators peak the late expansion phase wanes, which heralds a slowdown in growth.

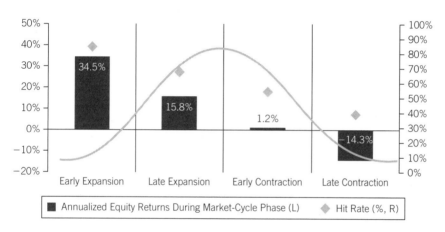

Figure 3.6   Equity Market Returns Lose Their Luster as the Business Cycle Matures
Source: Wolfe Trahan & Co.

Early contraction is when the economic outlook dims and investors begin to reduce their equity positions and flee to safer investment vehicles. In this phase of the cycle, market returns are typically subdued and sector leadership is dominated by inflation beneficiaries such as the energy, materials, and industrials sectors. This is the part of the cycle where inflationary pressures usually build, and monetary policy begins to tighten accordingly. The compounded forces of higher inflation and central bank tightening ultimately lead to an economic slowdown, or even a recession. During the early-contraction phase, investors should pay attention to early-cyclical groups as they are typically the ones that signal if the economy is headed for a reacceleration, a mid-cycle slowdown, or a recession.

This shift in leadership may also be an early warning that a top in equities is approaching. One of the canaries in the coal mine leading to the 2007 peak in equities was the underperformance of classic early-cyclical sectors. Consumer discretionary stocks peaked months before the general market, and passed the baton to the energy sector. The rising price of gasoline and the corresponding decline in consumer confidence shown in Figure 3.7 coincided with the change in sector leadership from consumer discretionary to energy.

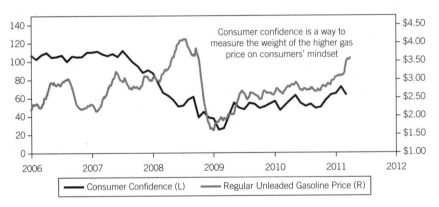

Figure 3.7   A Tipping Point Occurs When Gas Prices Begin to Weigh on Consumers
Source: Wolfe Trahan & Co.

If the slowdown intensifies, the cycle moves into the *late contraction* phase. Investors tend to take flight from cyclicality and move toward stability (counter-cyclical sectors) and assume a more defensive posture. At this point, sector leadership usually rotates into the stability of consumer staples, utilities, and health care stocks as highly economically sensitive cyclicals like financials[2] and technology fall out of favor. Selling of equities intensifies in the late contraction phase, and leading indicators prepare to bottom once again. The early and late contraction phases bring about, on average, equity returns of 1.2 percent and –14.3 percent, respectively.

The historical performance of cyclical versus counter-cyclical sectors when leading indicators are decelerating should play an important role in the sector-selection process. As shown in Figure 3.8, returns

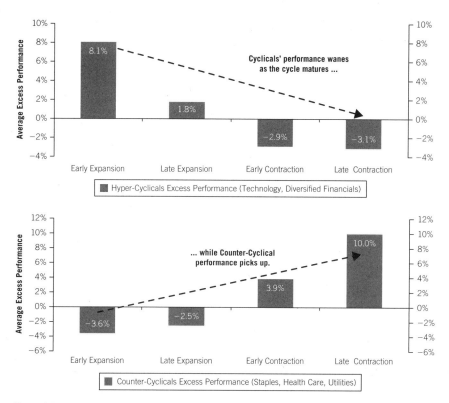

Figure 3.8   Equity Returns Are Mirror Images Across the Business Cycle
Source: Wolfe Trahan & Co.

during the waxing and waning of the business cycle are almost mirror images of each other.

Although many investors felt blindsided by the meltdown in the equity markets in 2008, the warning signs were there for those who looked. Equity performance followed historical business cycle patterns quite closely in the run-up to the bursting of the credit/ housing bubble. As the expansionary phase of the cycle drew to a close, consumer discretionary and financial stocks peaked in June of 2007—a full four months before the broader market top. Meanwhile, the energy sector continued to rally through the middle of May 2008. By that point, the S&P 500 index had already declined almost 10 percent from its October 2007 peak. The counter-cyclical consumer staples sector even managed to make a new high in September 2008, just prior to the S&P 500's plunge in the following months. Consumer staples, health care, and utilities were the top three performing sectors from the peak in the S&P 500 on October 9, 2007, through its trough on March 9, 2009. Incidentally, the equity market's low coincided with a bottom in leading indicators in March 2009, setting the stage for a new early expansion phase. Six months into the recovery, the pro-cyclical financial sector had gained more than 2.5 times the broader index, and almost 4.5 times the defensive consumer staples sector. Certainly hindsight is 20/20, but heeding the signals sent by macro forces at play in the markets could have helped investors better navigate this very challenging period.

Chapter Summary

- The cornerstone of a successful investment philosophy is the belief that leading economic indicators tend to be very good predictors of future economic activity. Combine with this the notion that stocks typically discount economic growth by about six months, and it is easy to see how equity markets are tightly correlated with leading economic indicators.
- Understanding the role of macro is more than just an academic exercise—it is the bedrock of successful investing. There is an enormous difference, however, between recognizing the importance of macro and learning how to interpret the stream of data to make better investment decisions.
- A solid understanding of the business cycle is crucial to benefit from the risk-reward shift as leading indicators peak or trough. The characteristics of a portfolio that outperforms during a period of deceleration in leading indicators are much different than those of a portfolio that outperforms as LEIs are accelerating.

The Pitfalls of Ignoring Macro Influences

Accidental Success

Markets are constantly in a state of uncertainty and flux and money is [made] by discounting the obvious and betting on the unexpected.[1]

—George Soros

Investors ignore the influence of macro on their portfolios for a variety of reasons, but almost always at their own peril. Commonly, this occurs when an investor's perception is skewed by "accidental success." Making a few correct calls using only a bottom-up strategy may influence investors to think that they are great stock pickers. In reality, it's more likely that they have just been on the right side of macro trends without realizing it, such as choosing stocks from a sector that was in favor. The dot-com bubble of the late 1990s was a perfect example of this phenomenon. It was a "throw a dart at the stock charts" era when everyone from taxi drivers to financial professionals had a profitable day-trading account. The successes fooled people into thinking that they were genius stock pickers, but in fact they were riding the wave of the tech revolution and mass speculation. This was a macro-driven story, albeit a bubble, but not a stock-picking market at all. Technology and telecomm stocks ruled the day. Almost any company with a "dot-com" at the end of its name had the potential to post exponential gains in a short period of time, regardless of the health (or even existence) of its balance sheet. When the fall came, it was indiscriminate as well. Technology companies with positive earnings growth and high-quality management were not spared the pain exacted on the sector as a whole. Tech giants such as Cisco and Oracle have yet, as of early 2011, to regain their highs reached in 2000. Top-down trends ruled both the rise and the fall of this market cycle.

Some successful investors may actually make decisions agnostic of macro influences, and merely benefit from a combination of good luck and timing. There are countless stories of hedge fund managers and traders who bet the farm on black and were lucky enough to have the roulette wheel reward their gamble—managers who shorted Enron on a bad feeling in the early 2000s or bet against subprime mortgages in 2007 using synthetic derivatives they did not even understand. Investors who follow winner-take-all strategies like these must make not only the correct directional call, but also pull the trigger at the right time. Even if an investor foresaw the potential carnage ahead in the real estate market—as François wrote about in 2005—putting that trade in motion too early could have wiped out a fund before the bubble actually burst. For each of the high-profile stories of hedge funds that made spectacular gains in 2007 and 2008, there are thousands of others that had the story right and the timing wrong. Using the context of the macro environment was the essential element that many of those unsuccessful managers missed.

Macro Lessons Are Learned through Experience

The signals sent by the business cycle before, during, and after the credit bubble are compelling examples of how macro trends can be used to navigate the equity markets. It is surprising that investors could be confronted with a powerful illustration such as this and still fail to embrace the influence of top-down trends. Memories are remarkably short in the financial industry, however, and like most life lessons they are better learned firsthand than by proxy. There is an incredible ability on Wall Street to believe that the pain exacted on other investors will not befall oneself. This belief is partially rooted in hubris, but partially due to the relatively short length of Wall Street careers. The make-it-big-and-get-out career path leaves 30 year olds calling the shots in more cases than the average person might imagine. Astute investors who are able to turn the massive losses experienced in 2008 into a lesson learned will be ahead of the pack when the next bubble arrives.

David Einhorn of Greenlight Capital—arguably most famous for shorting Lehman Brothers in 2007—told his personal tale of learning this lesson at the Value Investing Congress in October 2009. He referred to a speech he delivered in May 2005 at the Ira Sohn Investment Research Conference when he recommended MDC Holdings, a homebuilder, at $67 per share. The stock reached $89 within two months, but anyone who held on to the position rode it down with the rest of the sector in 2007. He said,

> Some of my MDC analysis was correct: it was less risky than its peers and would hold up better in a down cycle because it had less leverage and held less land. But this just meant that almost half a decade later, anyone who listened to me would have lost about 40 percent of his investment, instead of the 70 percent that the homebuilding sector lost.

The reason he gave for revisiting this story was that *it was not bad luck, but bad analysis.* He contrasted what he said that day with what he heard from legendary hedge fund manager Stan Druckenmiller a bit later in the conference. Stan's chosen topic was the grim story of the problems we faced from an expanding housing bubble inflated by a growing debt bubble. David wondered, even if Stan were correct, how would one translate such a big picture macro view into a successful investment strategy? He soon had the answer to his own question:

> I ignored Stan, rationalizing that even if he were right, there was no way to know when he would be right. This was an expensive error. *The lesson that I have learned is that it isn't reasonable to be agnostic about the big picture.* For years I had believed that I didn't need to take a view on the market or the economy because I considered myself to be a "bottom up" investor. Having my eyes open to the big picture doesn't mean abandoning stock picking, but it does mean managing the long-short exposure ratio more actively, worrying about what may be brewing in certain industries, and when appropriate, buying some just-in-case insurance for foreseeable macro risks even if they are hard to time.

David then proceeded to discuss the macro risks he believed were facing the markets at that point in late 2009. We couldn't have said it better ourselves.

Business Cycle Analysis Can Enhance the Power of Quant

Quantitative investment strategies have exploded in the last several decades as computing power became exponentially faster and cheaper. Everything from data mining to genetic algorithms has been employed to try to squeeze another few basis points of alpha from the markets. These types of strategies can, and do, work—quant models have played a huge role in successful investing over the last several decades. The most common problem is that very often managers blindly accept the output of these models without any qualitative judgment. Research shows that incorporating business cycle trends into quantitative analysis can greatly enhance its power.

Black box models based on broad historical data add little value at inflection points. Investors who rely solely on optimizers or other quantitative methodologies can end up loading up on what *has* worked, instead of investing for what is to come. Take the recent experience with the credit/housing bubble—it is unlikely that the same factors that add value in a cyclically driven market environment (led by consumer discretionary stocks and financials) would perform as well when moving into a defensive market environment (led by consumer staples and utilities). This was indeed the case. Tilting factors between cyclicality and stability added value as the market progressed through the cycle. The graph in Figure 4.1 shows how factor rotation played out over the past several years.

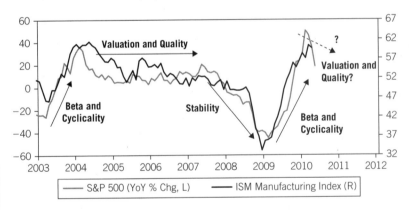

Figure 4.1   Factor Rotation in Past Cycles
Source: Wolfe Trahan & Co.

It is common sense that a strategy predicated on using history to predict future behavior falters when the future and the past diverge, but during every cycle managers crumble from blindly following these types of strategies. Using a macro overlay can improve results by directing investors toward the factors that work in the environment at hand. It can also turn a factor that appears to add no value into a very profitable input. Return on Assets (ROA) is a great example. The power of the business cycle becomes evident when timing the use of different factors. Based on the data shown in Figure 4.2, it appears that return on assets as a stand-alone factor adds value occasionally, but not in aggregate over the long term.

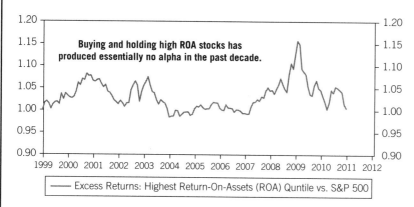

Figure 4.2   **Return on Equity Factor Appears to Deliver Zero Alpha in the Past Decade**
Source: Wolfe Trahan & Co.

When the return on assets factor is placed in the context of the business cycle, the picture becomes much clearer. Figure 4.3 highlights the value

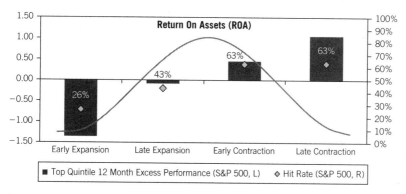

Figure 4.3   **Using Business Cycle Factor Rotation Shows That ROA Adds Value**
Source: Wolfe Trahan & Co.

(*continued*)

Business Cycle Analysis Can Enhance the Power of Quant (*Continued*)

added from ROA when used in the contraction phases of the business cycle. Waiting to incorporate ROA as a factor until the peak in leading indicators leads to outperformance 63 percent of the time. Conversely, 74 percent of the time, investing in stocks with the highest return on assets in the early expansion phase of the cycle leads to market underperformance.

Chapter Summary

- Investors ignore the influence of macro on their portfolios for a variety of reasons, but almost always at their own peril.
- The dot-com bubble of the late 1990s was a perfect example of accidental success. The successes fooled people into thinking that they were genius stock pickers, but in fact they were riding the wave of the tech revolution and mass speculation.
- Some successful investors may actually make decisions agnostic of macro influences, and merely benefit from a combination of good luck and timing.
- The signals sent by the business cycle before, during, and after the credit bubble are compelling examples of how macro trends can be used to navigate the equity markets. It is surprising that investors could be confronted with a powerful illustration such as this and still fail to embrace the influence of top-down trends.

PART
II

THE ROOTS OF THE NEW ERA OF UNCERTAINTY: THE CREDIT CRISIS

Proximity can be both good and bad for understanding the severity of a situation. Closeness can provide access to information, but it can also cause distortions in perception. No one had a clearer picture of the creation of the housing and credit bubble than policy makers at the Federal Reserve, yet they were among the most adamant deniers that a problem existed. They repeatedly claimed that the rise in housing prices was completely justified by the economic backdrop, despite clear signs of speculative excess. Many analysts on Wall Street agreed with the Fed's assessment, or at least took advantage of it. It's possible that they too were suffering from far-sightedness, or else they merely rode the wave of profits with little regard for long-term consequences. Regardless, the behavior by Wall Street that fed the bubble, and the lack of ability or willingness of policy makers to acknowledge it, has called into question the judgment of both of these groups.

Looking back at this bubble, a couple of very important pieces of information are revealed. First, in the context of an historical macro framework, the bubble was predictable. Second, and more disturbing, given that the telltale signs of a bubble environment were so apparent, investors in the future must be more skeptical of relying on the words and actions of the Federal Reserve to determine the risks in the economy. Bubbles are serial in nature, and therefore investors must be prepared to use the historical framework to recognize and avoid future manias with little help from either Wall Street or Washington, D.C.

CHAPTER 5

A View from the Front Lines

It's not denial. I'm just selective about the reality I accept.[1]

—Bill Waterson

The explosion of the housing bubble in 2008 turned the financial world upside down. Despite how obvious the excesses in housing and credit now appear, during the years before the meltdown many people were skeptical that a bubble existed at all. There was a lively debate in the financial press, but many Wall Street strategists, and even Federal Reserve bankers, rationalized the extreme run-up in housing prices. They saw the accelerating housing market as justified by the sustained low level of interest rates, but *those low rates were precisely why housing was in a bubble.* Take, for example, a paper entitled "Are Home Prices the Next 'Bubble'?" published by two economists from the Federal Reserve Bank of New York in December 2004. Their resounding conclusion was that no bubble existed in the housing market. (The views expressed are those of the authors and do not necessarily reflect the position of the Federal Reserve Bank of New York or the Federal Reserve System. The Federal Reserve Bank of New York provides no warranty, express or implied, as to the accuracy, timeliness, completeness, merchantability, or fitness for any particular purpose of any information contained in documents produced and provided by the Federal Reserve Bank of New York in any form or manner whatsoever.)

> Our analysis of the U.S. housing market in recent years finds little evidence to support the existence of a national home

price bubble. Rather, it appears that home prices have risen in line with increases in personal income and declines in nominal interest rates. Moreover, expectations of rapid price appreciation do not appear to be a major factor behind the strong housing market. Our observations also suggest that home prices are not likely to plunge in response to deteriorating fundamentals to the extent envisioned by some analysts. Real home prices have been less volatile than other asset prices, such as equity prices.

"Are Home Prices the Next 'Bubble'?,"
Jonathan McCarthy and Richard W. Peach,
FRBNY Economic Policy Review,
Vol. 10, No. 3, December 2004

Adamant *bubble denial* extended well beyond staff economists at the Federal Reserve. It reached the highest echelons of the policy-setting Federal Open Market Committee—many of the same policy makers who played a major part in creating the bubble! Ben Bernanke, who took over as Fed Chairman in 2005 from Alan Greenspan, reiterated on many occasions the conclusions of the research paper quoted above. In 2005, Chairman Bernanke talked down the likelihood that housing was in a bubble saying, "We've never had a decline in housing prices on a nationwide basis."[2] Once the cracks in the housing market were obvious, he was still denying that the weakness would extend beyond real estate. In March 2007 he asserted, "At this juncture, however, the impact on the broader economy and financial markets of the problems in the subprime market seems likely to be contained."[3] As late as 2008, Chairman Bernanke was still not convinced of the severity of the situation: "The Federal Reserve is not currently forecasting a recession."[4]

As chief investment strategist at Bear Stearns, François saw things differently, even during those early years. He and his team had written a special report on bubbles in June 2005 that caused discomfort inside the bank. In the report, they explored the history of asset bubbles dating back to the tulip mania in seventeenth century Holland, and explained the factors common to bubble environments. The goal of the report was only to provide investors with a framework to identify and profit from a bubble in the making, and learn to avoid the inevitable meltdown. The actual result was somewhat of a controversy in the ranks of the Research Division's management at Bear Stearns. The bank had significant and growing

Table 5.1   Summing Up the Bubble Benchmarks—June 2005

Characteristics of a Bubble-Prone Backdrop	Has This Occurred?	Conditions Present at Bubble Peak	Has This Occurred?
1) Easy Money	1/2 Yes	5) Speculation	Yes
2) Strong Economic Growth	Yes	6) Yield Spreads Widen	No
3) Prosperity	Yes	7) Pricing Pressures Accelerate	Yes
4) Pricing Pressures Build	Yes	8) Short Rates Rise	Yes
		9) Yield Curve Flattens	Yes
		10) Business Activity Slows	Yes
Score:	3.5/4		5/6

Source: "Asset Bubbles: A Look at Past and Future Manias," Bear Stearns Equity Research, Investment Strategy, June 2005

exposure to the housing market, which later spelled demise for the company in early 2008. Management was not sure how to handle its chief strategist publishing research counter to some of the bank's then-most-profitable investments.

One conclusion in François' report was that the economy in 2005 exhibited eight and a half out of the ten characteristics typical of a bubble-prone environment, suggesting readiness for an asset bubble to burst. Table 5.1 shows the 10 Bubble Benchmarks and their status in June 2005.

After showing in detail how the economic landscape supported the likelihood of a bubble, François and team then proposed that the sector most likely to experience an imminent correction was real estate. The low-interest-rate environment that Federal Reserve officials so often cited had made housing extremely affordable with interest rates at 40-year lows. That was the good news. The bad news was that a huge diversification in mortgage offerings in recent years and the steep yield curve, which allowed banks to lend very profit-ably, had led to a frenzy of *speculation* in mortgage lending. Figure 5.1 shows the soaring number of houses for sale on which building had not even started.

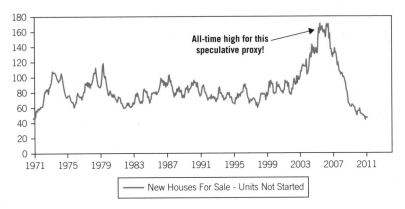

Figure 5.1   New Houses for Sale—Units Not Started
Source: Wolfe Trahan & Co.

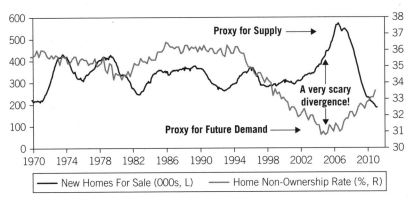

Figure 5.2   Increasing Supply Plus Shrinking Demand Equals Eventual Imbalance!
Source: Wolfe Trahan & Co.

Homeowners were more leveraged than ever. The share of households' mortgage obligations to owners' equity was at a 25-year high. At the same time, the yield curve was beginning to flatten as the Fed raised short-term rates and the longer-dated end of the yield curve did not move. This indicated an impending tightening of lending conditions at banks. Removal of the massive low-interest-rate tailwind, combined with highly leveraged households, signaled a rough road ahead for the housing market. There was also a growing disconnection between the outlook for real estate market growth and the housing supply/demand balance. Figure 5.2 shows the supply of new homes increasing at the same time that the share of people who did not already own a home was near an all-time low, and still declining. The conclusion was that a deteriorating supply/demand balance, tightening credit, and over-leveraged homeowners presented a very poor risk/reward profile for the asset class.

Reactions were tense, both from Bear Stearns colleagues and clients. An email typical of some clients' responses was sent to François and his boss, the Director of Research, and consisted of name-calling and questioning François' experience. This particular client had been in the business a long time, and felt strongly that housing prices would go up indefinitely since that was the way it had "always" happened.

Once the report was published, some factions at Bear decided to make profitable lemonade out of lemons. The report gave the Bear Stearns Derivatives team the idea to create a structured note designed to return *double the inverse return of the homebuilders index;* in other words, it would profit if the construction industry fell into decline. The derivative product was marketed with a coffee mug printed with a tongue-in-cheek slogan, *"Mr. Housing Bubble, if I pop you're screwed."* Some would argue that the firm was less concerned with presenting the right view to its clients than with profiting from whatever direction the market took.

The Bubble Intensifies

In May 2006, François revisited the controversial housing bubble in a report entitled "Approaching an Inflection Point in the Bubble Cycle." Macro developments over the previous year only confirmed his belief that real estate was ripe for a meltdown. The lending frenzy had intensified and mortgage lending stories became more and more surreal. It was not uncommon for a homebuyer to obtain a $500,000 mortgage including fees, sometimes even with a cash payout for furniture purchases, without verifiable income! People were snapping up this free money for multiple homes and pooling resources to speculate in some of the most "desirable" locations such as Las Vegas and South Florida. Speculative lending accelerated as non-traditional lenders (in other words, mortgage brokers) were pushing more-conservative banks and savings and loans to the backburner. These mortgage lenders were incentivized to make as many loans as possible since they just packaged them up and passed them along to investors as mortgage backed securities. Enthusiastic speculators had all of the credit they could want, and banks eagerly snatched up loans to repackage into profitable securities.

In stark contrast to Chairman Bernanke's assertion in 2007 that any damage done to the real estate market would remain contained, an entire year earlier François posited that the unwinding of the real estate bubble could broadly impact financial markets for years to come.

> The speed with which the housing bubble deflates will have important implications for household spending and could determine how quickly and strongly the Fed increases liquidity again.
>
> *"Approaching an Inflection Point in the Bubble Cycle,"*
> Bear Stearns Investment Strategy, May 2006

The point is not that all of the market calls made by François and his team were correct, but merely that the Fed was extremely short sighted in its views, and officials were unwilling to apply the lessons learned from previous bubbles.

The irony is that in the environment that fuels bubble psychology—imprudent attitudes of extreme optimism regarding economic expansion, general prosperity, and perceived liquidity—it is extremely difficult for investors to recognize the pitfalls. At this point in the housing bubble, the exuberance in the real estate market still was too frothy and credulous for most investors to imagine that a financial disaster was looming. This excessively optimistic viewpoint is the foundation for the "it's different this time" belief inherent in bubbles. Even among investors who believed that parts of the market were overextended, many thought they were somehow immune. In 2006, many market observers were aware that hot property locations like South Florida and California were overheated, but denied the mania could migrate away from the coasts. In a series of questions and answers addressing misconceptions about bubbles, François asked, *"Why should I worry about a potential real estate bubble in California if I live in Iowa?"* The answer was,

> Because it is important to remember that asset bubbles frequently begin as localized events, yet their ramifications often rattle the

broader markets and sometimes the entire economy. A bubble can form in a single asset class, stock market industry, or geographic region and boil over to impact a multitude of industries and often the entire financial landscape.

"Approaching an Inflection Point in the Bubble Cycle,"
Bear Stearns Investment Strategy, May 2006

Unfortunately, this was exactly what happened in the years after his controversial report was published. Within two years of publication, the entirety of Bear Stearns was paying the price for ignoring the forecasts of its chief investment strategist. François left the organization in February 2007, a year before Bear Stearns collapsed, to join an independent research boutique.

Slaying of the Bear

During the boom years, Bear Stearns had underwritten a sizable volume of securities backed by mortgages classified as subprime and Alt-A.[5] These types of mortgages were more risky than typical conforming, or prime, mortgages because they were obtained by people with low and/or risky credit ratings, sometimes with little or no money committed for a down payment. These mortgages often have a higher default rate than prime mortgages. Bear Stearns, the fifth-largest U.S. investment bank, and many other Wall Street banks, bundled these loans together into mortgage backed securities and then claimed that the whole was worth more than the sum of the parts. In other words, a bundle of subprime loans could have had an AAA credit rating even though the individual mortgages were of much lower quality. The reasoning was that by packaging the loans together, the risk of default on any significant portion of the loans was reduced. Bankers were both flouting basic lending principles and ignoring the macro influences that could and would take down the housing market as a whole. Credit rating agencies were happy to provide high-quality ratings as they competed for the banks' lucrative mortgage-backed-securities business. It was easy for the financial community to view these securities through rose-colored glasses since the market was enormous and highly profitable. The size of the mortgage backed securities market grew from $3.6 trillion in 2000 to $9.1 trillion by 2007.[6]

The first cracks at the firm appeared in 2007 when the troubles in the subprime mortgage market began to accumulate and accelerate. In the early months of the year, Bear Stearns' two largest hedge funds were declining rapidly due to their exposure to the increasingly shaky subprime market. Facing massive redemptions and margin calls, the managers of the funds chose to hide the growing problems from investors until the weight of the markets forced their hands; the funds were shuttered in the summer of 2007. Although monthly performance summaries distributed by the funds indicated that direct subprime exposure was in the neighborhood of 6 to 8 percent of each portfolio, *after the collapse of Bear Stearns it was learned that total subprime exposure was approximately 60 percent.*[7] Losses to fund investors were significant, and investors in Bear's stock were now on high alert.

The following spring, the entire house of cards came tumbling down. Deteriorating credit markets led to large write-offs for the bank. In a single day, Moody's downgraded 160 tranches of mortgage backed securities that Bear had underwritten.[8] Clients and counterparties feared that Bear was in the throes of a severe liquidity crisis and did not have enough cash to continue operating. On the morning of March 10, 2008, a run on the stock price of Bear Stearns began as market players bet that the bank was insolvent. Within days, emergency negotiations between the bank and Treasury officials led to JPMorgan Chase offering just $2 a share to purchase Bear. The final price was upped to $10, still a far cry from the $170-per-share level near which the stock traded just over a year before its collapse.

An avalanche of shareholder lawsuits and federal investigations followed the collapse of Bear. A core question in many of these cases was how the bank's management failed to see the impending housing crisis when its chief investment strategist had been pounding the table about it for several years. The answer that no one will hear in a court of law is that the profits were just too attractive to pass up. In the end, however, management's dismissal of the 2005 and 2006 research reports on the housing bubble cost them, and many investors, a great deal.

Chapter Summary

- Adamant denial of a housing bubble permeated the Federal Reserve in the mid-2000s. Policy makers published research concluding that there was little evidence of a national home price bubble, and attributed the rise to increases in personal income and declines in nominal interest rates.

- François was chief investment strategist at Bear Stearns during that period. He published two special reports on bubbles in 2005 and 2006 concluding that the economy in 2005 exhibited eight and a half out of the 10 characteristics typical of a bubble-prone environment.

- The good news was that housing was extremely affordable with interest rates at 40-year lows. The bad news was that a huge diversification in mortgage offerings in recent years and a steepening yield curve, which allowed banks to lend very profitably, had led to a frenzy of speculation in mortgage lending.

- Early in 2007, cracks began to appear in Bear Stearns' two largest hedge funds due to subprime bond market exposure. This event alerted investors to broader problems at Bear, and by the following spring deteriorating credit markets led to large writeoffs.

- Clients and counterparties feared that Bear was in the throes of a severe liquidity crisis. On the morning of March 10, 2008, a run began on Bear Stearns' stock price and within days the bank had been sold to JP Morgan Chase for $10 a share.

CHAPTER 6

In the Weeds

It ain't what you don't know that gets you into trouble. It's what you know for sure that just ain't so.[1]

—Mark Twain

There are two ways to think about the massive failure by Wall Street banks to anticipate the housing and credit debacle. One is that they really didn't understand the exposure their firms had to these highly risky assets. The second is that they did understand, at least to some degree, and yet failed or chose not to act. Neither view inspires trust, and leaves people with the choice of regarding the banks as either incredibly ignorant or supremely greedy. A cornerstone concept of the new era of uncertainty is this lack of trust in the financial industry.

Reality likely has a foot in both these camps. There were many traders, brokers, hedge fund managers, and even CEOs who did not understand the housing bubble was not just a bull market—the bubble expansion was rooted in an easy-credit mania. Years of extremely easy monetary policy laid the foundation for abuse of credit that permeated not only the housing market, but many facets of Americans' lives. Housing was only the most visible, most speculative manifestation of overindulgence. People who thought the excesses were manageably confined to the subprime real estate market did not understand the macro implications of a credit crisis. Some in the financial industry clearly saw the growing financial market contradictions and avoided the crash. Many others, however, could not resist dipping into the punch bowl despite already being drunk.

Both the ignorant and greedy arguments can be partially attributed to being "too deep in the weeds." Like parents unaware of their children's faults, or Congressmen bogged down in the minutia of Washington politics, living and working in the all-encompassing world of a Wall Street bank can greatly distort one's perspective. Long hours spent with the same people who read the same research and watch the same financial television coverage can skew group-wide opinions in the same direction. Just as the social reinforcement of a bubble-building process can fuel its growth, repeated discussions of a market view by similar-minded people can lend an opinion even more credibility. Perpetuating a profitable investment strategy also can be tempting when that house in the Hamptons is within reach. As long as the party continues so do the bonuses, introducing a confirmation bias as analysts rely only on the information that supports their views.

The uncertainty and volatility of financial markets also contribute to the confusion. Forecasting market trends is far from an exact science, and staying in the game a little longer is tempting even when the eventual outcome is increasingly likely and clear. The longer the market remains irrational, the easier it is to convince oneself that a new paradigm actually has arrived.

Neurophysiologists, who research cognitive functions, have found that people driven by emotion can suffer decision impairment similar to people with certain types of brain injuries.[2] This may occur in rabid sports fans, political ideologues, and certainly investors. An intense emotional interest causes one to selectively perceive events. Data that contradicts the predisposed opinion are ignored, and even memory can be affected as the afflicted selectively retain what supports the view, and mask any memories that conflict.

The Fog of War

The ambiguities and uncertainties of investing through a manic period in the markets are similar to what has been coined as the "fog of war." This term has been in the media recently with respect to the United States' military actions abroad, but the concept dates back to Prussian military analyst Carl von Clausewitz who wrote,

> Lastly, the great uncertainty of all data in war is a peculiar difficulty, because all action must, to a certain extent, be planned

in a mere twilight, which in addition not infrequently—like the effect of a fog or moonshine—gives to things exaggerated dimensions and unnatural appearance.

Carl von Clausewitz, On War *from the*
Project Gutenberg E-book,
Book II, Chapter II

Von Clausewitz refers to the opacity of information and the resulting uncertainty that soldiers experience in assessing a situation during military operations. Misjudgments about the surroundings, the enemy's capabilities and goals, and even a soldier's own skills can lead to errors in execution. The same may be said for the war being fought in the capital markets. Working day to day in the weeds of the financial markets can cloud judgment in the moment. Using historical macro trends as a guide can help maintain perspective, avoid complacency, and prevent extreme extrapolation from current conditions.

The Fog of War: Eleven Lessons from the Life of Robert S. McNamara is a documentary film made about the life of the former United States Secretary of Defense.[3] The movie elaborates on 11 lessons about war-time decision making drawn from interviews with McNamara, whose career grew from World War II military officer to Defense Secretary for Presidents Kennedy and Johnson, and spanned both the Cuban Missile Crisis and the Vietnam War. The lessons that McNamara learned during his years in and around the battlefield

---

Lessons for Investors from *The Fog of War*

1. Empathize with your enemy.
   Investors' primary enemies are slow growth, high inflation, and the Fed's boom-bust policy approach to fighting these enemies.

2. Rationality will not save us.
   Clinging blindly to what "should" be happening will not always position an investor on the profitable side of the market. In other words, "The market can stay irrational longer than you can stay solvent."—John Maynard Keynes.[4]

3. There's something beyond one's self.
   Look beyond the obvious to add value. Despite evidence that macro forces play the dominant role in determining equity returns, most investors remain bottom-up focused.

(continued)

Lessons for Investors from *The Fog of War* (*Continued*)

4. Maximize efficiency.
   Maximize risk-adjusted reward, not just reward.

5. Proportionality should be a guideline in war.
   A response should be proportional to the situation it addresses, but investors as well as policy makers tend to overshoot the target.

6. Get the data.
   Don't rely on instinct, learn the lessons of history, and understand what data is important and when.

7. Belief and seeing are often both wrong.
   Look under the hood and be wary of following the crowd. Correlation is not causation.

8. Be prepared to reexamine your reasoning.
   Constantly reassess an investment thesis in the context of the environment. Never dismiss the possibility that your view is wrong.

9. In order to do good, you may have to engage in evil.
   Policies that are painful in the short term—such as austerity measures and tax increases—can end up being beneficial for investors in the long term.

10. Never say never.
    Don't believe that something will *always* happen, and don't believe that something will *never* happen.

11. You can't change human nature.
    Bubbles are serial in nature, and each generation will create new bubble cycles. Investors tend to overshoot and policy makers overreact.

were largely about questioning and looking beyond the obvious. These are mental exercises that many investors fail to perform, but could prove to be invaluable. Above is a reinterpretation of *The Fog of War's* 11 lessons for investors.

Lessons the Fed Could Have Learned from the Fog of War

Several of the 11 lessons that McNamara learned as a key advisor to American military policy could have been applied by the Federal Reserve, and Chairman Bernanke, in response to the recession. There is a striking parallel to the experiences of the two leaders, who both managed under crisis and through multiple presidential administrations. Indeed, both men have been at the helm of decision-making at a time when the country was inches away from devastation . . . one nuclear and the other financial.

The first lesson that the Fed could have benefited from learning is number five: "Proportionality should be a guideline in war." As McNamara was quoted in the documentary film *The Fog of War: Eleven Lessons from the Life of Robert S. McNamara*:

> Proportionality should be a guideline in war. Killing 50% to 90% of the people of 67 Japanese cities and then bombing them with two nuclear bombs is not proportional, in the minds of some people, to the objectives we were trying to achieve.

In the wake of the financial crisis, there is no debate that there was a need for unprecedented stimulus. The question is whether the Fed exceeded an appropriately scaled policy decision. In his infamous November 21, 2002, speech before the National Economists Club, "Deflation: Making sure 'it' doesn't happen here," then-Fed-Governor Ben Bernanke discussed how policy makers could ensure that deflation does not make its way onto American shores. He identified seven specific actions that the Central Bank could take, all of which have been put into practice since the onset of the financial crisis (see Table 6.1). The question that has yet to be answered is, Was this fire-bombing policy response proportional to the crisis? The initial effects of quantitative easing have lifted markets, but the secondary effects, such as inflation, may result in a longer-term headwind for both equities and the economy.

The next important lesson for the Fed should have been that "Belief and seeing are both often wrong." In the fog of war, combatants often see what they want to see and believe what they want to believe in order to rationalize the decisions they make. The same often holds true in the investment process as investors' beliefs sometimes become self-fulfilling prophecies. There is little doubt that the Fed's injection of $600 billion of new money into the economy during the second round of quantitative easing had an effect on financial markets. There is doubt, however, about the extent to which markets were already set to recover on the back of improving economic data well before Chairman Bernanke even hinted at additional liquidity.

Looking back at the environment leading up to the August 2010 speech in Jackson Hole when Chairman Bernanke announced

Table 6.1   The Bernanke Doctrine: Policy Actions to Avoid Deflation, as Explained by Ben Bernanke

Policy Action	Explanation in Bernanke's 2002 Speech
1. Increase the money supply.	". . . the U.S. government has a technology, called a printing press . . . that allows it to produce as many U.S. dollars as it wishes at essentially no cost."
2. Ensure liquidity makes its way into the financial system through a variety of measures.	". . . the U.S. government is not going to print money and distribute it willy-nilly (although as we will see later, there are practical policies that approximate this behavior)."
3. Lower interest rates to 0 percent.	". . . under a fiat (that is, paper) money system, a government . . . should always be able to generate increased nominal spending and inflation, even when the short-term nominal interest rate is at zero. . . . A more direct method, which I personally prefer, would be for the Fed to begin announcing explicit ceilings for yields on longer-maturity Treasury debt. . . ."
4. Control the yield on corporate bonds and other privately issued securities.	". . . the Fed [could] offer fixed-term loans to banks at low or zero interest, with a wide range of private assets (including, among others, corporate bonds, commercial paper, bank loans, and mortgages) deemed eligible as collateral. . . . Pursued aggressively, such a program could significantly reduce liquidity and term premiums on the assets used as collateral. Reductions in these premiums would lower the cost of capital both to banks and the nonbank private sector, over and above the beneficial effect already conferred by lower interest rates on government securities."
5. Depreciate the U.S. dollar.	"A striking example from U.S. history is Franklin Roosevelt's 40 percent devaluation of the dollar against gold in 1933-34. . . . The devaluation and the rapid increase in money supply . . . ended the U.S. deflation remarkably quickly."
6. Execute a *de facto* depreciation by buying foreign currencies on a massive scale.	". . . the Fed has the authority to buy foreign government debt, as well as domestic government debt. Potentially, this class of assets offers huge scope for Fed operations, as the quantity of foreign assets eligible for purchase by the Fed is several times the stock of U.S. government debt."
7. Buy industries throughout the U.S. economy with "newly created money."	". . . the government could increase spending on current goods and services or even acquire existing real or financial assets. If the Treasury issued debt to purchase private assets and the Fed then purchased an equal amount of Treasury debt with newly created money, the whole operation would be the economic equivalent of direct open-market operations in private assets."

Source: "Deflation: Making sure 'it' doesn't happen here," Ben Bernanke, Remarks before the National Economists Club, Washington, D.C., November 21, 2002

a second round of quantitative easing, it is clear that there were several factors already in place to promote a rally in stocks. In other words, more quantitative easing was not the sole catalyst for the subsequent equity rally, nor was it even the primary influence. At the time, many anticipatory indicators pointed to an imminent rise in leading indicators, including slowing inflation, rising money flow indicators, and a shift toward early cyclical sectors outperforming late-stage cyclicals. Chairman Bernanke and the investing public may have let their preconceived beliefs lead them to apply causality to a relationship, which just was not true—an equity rally driven by quantitative easing instead of the macro backdrop.

The lesson that policy makers (arguably) most egregiously ignored during the housing bubble and its aftermath was, "Never say never." Throughout each stage of the housing bubble, policy makers in the United States held firmly to the belief that there was no bubble, and that house prices were set to resume their upward trajectory. Incredibly, in October 2002, Chairman Bernanke gave a speech to the National Association for Business Economics in which he named the rapid growth of credit as an indicator of bubbles.

"A situation develops in which institutions can directly or indirectly take speculative positions using funds protected by the deposit insurance safety net—the classic "heads I win, tails you lose" situation. When this moral hazard is present, credit flows rapidly into inelastically supplied assets, such as real estate."
—*Ben Bernanke, "Asset-Price Bubbles and Monetary Policy," Remarks before the New York Chapter of the National Association for Business Economics, New York, October 15, 2002*

This wisdom was nowhere to be found just five years later when the Federal Reserve was facing the reality of this situation.

The Bubble Was Predictable!

Investors *not* too deep in the weeds could see that the housing bubble was predictable and avoidable. The playbook was familiar. Like all other bubbles throughout the history of markets, ample access to credit drove its inflation. An accommodative Federal Reserve and a powerful fiscal package put in place to recharge the economy in the aftermath of the 2001 market collapse led to a massive expansion of credit. Easy money fueled confidence, which in turn engendered speculation. When interest rates began heading higher in 2005, it was only a matter of time before credit dried up and the bubble inevitably popped.

The conditions for a bubble were firmly in place, but an accommodative monetary backdrop does not actually indicate which asset class is ripe for bubble-dom. There were, however, a variety of other factors that clearly pointed toward real estate.

Media Frenzy

Bubbles can generate massive amounts of wealth, and where there is money to be made the media is never far behind. Historically, one of the best qualitative measures of a bubble has been how prevalent the subject is in the media. By 2006, web sites specializing in bringing together parties interested in real estate flipping were commonplace, boasting taglines such as "Bubbles Are for Bathtubs."[5] On television, *Flip This House* followed a team of renovators as they bought properties, fixed them up, and flipped them for a profit. A book called *The Automatic Millionaire Homeowner: A Powerful Plan to Finish Rich in Real Estate* chided anyone who did *not* own real estate as foolish in an environment where access to credit was so simple.

Aside from the cultural indications of a bubble in real estate, there were also a number of quantitative factors that pointed in the same direction.

Stretched Valuation

There were a number of ways to gauge the frothiness of the housing market, but valuation was a very easy starting point. Both home sales prices and rental prices were stretched individually, but looking at them on a relative basis, as shown in Figure 6.1, was alarming. In 2006, the ratio of mean sales price to the mean rental price was at its highest level in more than two decades, implying that buying was far more expensive than renting.

Another way to measure how stretched real estate valuation had become was to look at the deviation of home prices from income. The chart in Figure 6.2 shows the standard deviation of the value of new homes for sale relative to employee compensation. This in

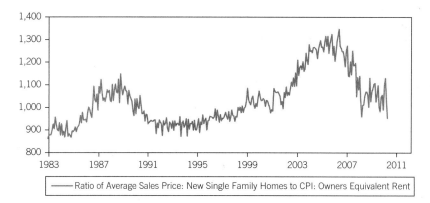

Figure 6.1   Home Sale Prices Far More Stretched Than Rental Prices
Source: Wolfe Trahan & Co.

Figure 6.2   Real Estate Met the Speculative Criteria: A Move Beyond Fundamentals
Source: Wolfe Trahan & Co.

essence compared the price of a home to the means available to buy one. Not since the late 1970s had this measure reached such heights!

Signs of Speculation

Signs of speculation were also a way to identify housing as the bubble du jour. The number of new houses for sale that were not yet under construction was a terrific indicator of speculative demand. Speculation in the housing market, as measured by this series, had never been so high. Similar to the tulip bulbs that were yet to bloom, people were buying homes for which the foundation was not yet laid. This level of speculation was particularly precarious in light of homeowners' difficulties in meeting their already existing mortgage obligation.

Breadth of Participation

A frothy asset market cannot truly be called a bubble unless it is a widespread phenomenon. The chart shown in Figure 6.3 was important in identifying that the housing bubble was indeed a nationwide event, and not confined to the east and west coasts. The percentage of states experiencing well-above average levels of home price appreciation was the highest it had been in several decades. The national scope of rising prices indicated that a housing slow-down would have far-reaching effects.

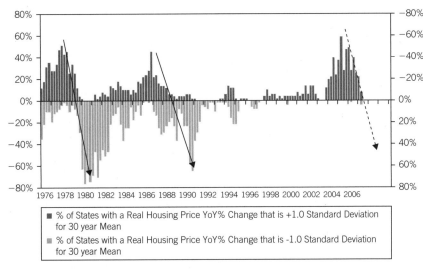

Figure 6.3   Housing Boom Is a Geographically Widespread Phenomenon
Source: Wolfe Trahan & Co.

Supply/Demand Imbalance

Understanding the fundamentals of supply and demand for a market is key to gauging whether or not there is an imbalance. Not only was supply skyrocketing, but the rate of home non-ownership—in other words, potential demand—was declining sharply. The chart in Figure 6.4 shows how strong the increase in housing supply had

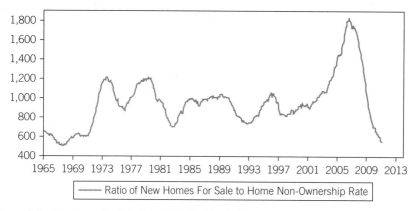

Figure 6.4   New Homes for Sale (Supply) Divided by the Home Non-Ownership Rate (Demand)
Source: Wolfe Trahan & Co.

been relative to demand. The discrepancy was far greater than anything seen in several decades.

And the End Was Foreseeable . . . Macro Could Have Helped

The quantitative and qualitative indicators clearly pointed toward a bubble in real estate, which in and of itself was not a sign to race for the exits. Bubbles can prove very profitable for an extended period. Changes in the monetary policy backdrop, however, predicted that the end was near. Just as easy money sparks the growth of a bubble, a move toward less-accommodative conditions often heralds its demise. Monetary policy takes time to filter through the economic system, so when the Fed began raising rates in 2004 alarm bells did not sound. As Figure 6.5 shows, however, after about two years of rising interest rates the stage was set for tighter credit conditions to choke off the speculative frenzy in housing.

History as a Guide

To paraphrase Mark Twain, history may not repeat itself, but macro trends that herald the creation and destruction of a bubble do rhyme. Figure 6.6 lays out the common signposts in a bubble cycle. Unique catalysts usually set the mania in motion, but understanding the conditions critical for a bubble environment to develop is crucial.

Using macro trends to identify where we are in the economic framework can also help determine when a bubble is long in the

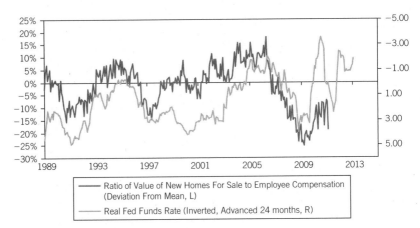

Figure 6.5   How the Imbalance Eventually Unfolds
Source: Wolfe Trahan & Co.

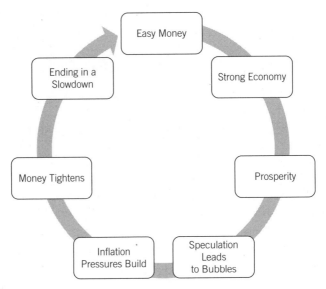

Figure 6.6   The Lifecycle of a Bubble
Source: Wolfe Trahan & Co.

tooth. Ample liquidity resulting from sustained low interest rates encourages investors to move toward riskier assets. The easing trends in monetary policy that predated the housing boom played out similarly before the technology run-up in the late 1990s. Figure 6.7 shows how trends in monetary policy dovetailed with the creation and destruction of bubbles during the last several decades.

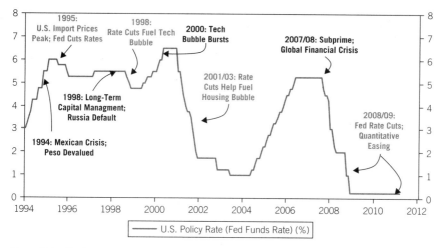

Figure 6.7   The Serial Nature of Bubbles
Source: Wolfe Trahan & Co.

On the other side of the coin, higher interest rates lead to an eventual tightening of credit conditions, and indicate that a bubble's days are numbered. Just a few years ago, energy stocks experienced a condensed bubble that was ignited and doused by these predictable macro patterns. As the Fed aggressively lowered rates starting in the fall of 2007, the dollar fell and propelled the price of oil higher. A weaker dollar makes commodities like oil, priced in dollars, more expensive on the global market. Energy stocks rallied, even as the broad market declined, as analysts predicted oil would reach prices of $300 to $400 per barrel. Despite a weakening global economy, Figure 6.8 shows that the soaring price of oil prompted several central banks to raise rates, which contributed to breaking the back of the energy stock rally.

Despite the consistency of bubble signposts, the revisionist thinking that stems from bubble psychology is powerful. This is precisely the time, however, when it is most important to look back at history's lessons. A manic environment is one of optimism and over-confidence. The idea of financial disaster is so remote that is it easily dismissed, and almost all developments are viewed in a positive light. Some of the most outrageous cases of bubble psychology in the past several hundred years have occurred in countries undergoing major industrial or technological revolutions. The series of railroad bubbles during

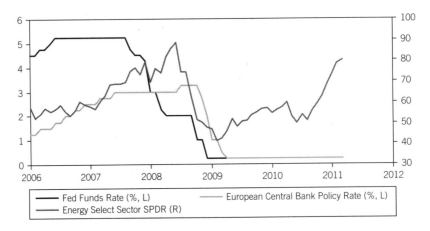

Figure 6.8   The Fed Sparks an Oil Rally
Source: Wolfe Trahan & Co., Sector Select SPDR, Yahoo! Finance

the 1800s, or the dot-com bubble come to mind. These countries often enjoy a dominant position in trade and financial markets as well, enhancing the belief that a new era has arrived. The psychology of endless prosperity, also known as the "it's different this time" belief, brings with it a change in the perception of risk and a call for new ways to value assets.

Think back to a well-known bubble when a new era was supposedly upon us. The premise of the new age was the elimination of the business cycle, since new technologies and innovations were dramatically changing the business landscape forever. Better corporate management improved productivity and inventory control. Interest rates were low, liquidity was ample, and stocks soared to levels 30 times income. Former, more conservative valuation metrics were eschewed in favor of discounting future earnings. It was widely believed that this new economy would end the boom/bust cycle, promote steady growth in wealth and savings, and lead to continuously rising stock prices.[6]

Two years before the market peak, speculation was running rampant and stock market margin debt was at an historical high. At this time, the Federal Reserve eased monetary policy in response to currency troubles in foreign economies. Rates were lowered to avert a worldwide financial crisis, sending liquidity, margin debt, and stock prices higher for another two years.

This story may sound like a retelling of the go-go days of the internet bubble in the late 1990s, but it is actually the scenario that played out in 1928 to 1929 prior to the Great Depression! Clearly, the idea of new era economics is not a modern invention.

Policy Makers Behind the Curve

It's not uncommon for policy makers to move in the wrong direction, as they did when they lowered rates instead of raising them in the late-1920s and 1990s. They often are averse to addressing potential problems before they occur, and then deny the severity when they actually happen. Implied support from senior policy officials only serves to reinforce the optimism of bubble psychology. Former Federal Reserve Chairman Alan Greenspan, who presided over the creation and destruction of the technology bubble, has argued that it is impossible to know an asset price bubble has developed until after it has burst.[7] Obviously, policy makers also suffer from the fog of war.

Both Chairman Greenspan and current Chairman Ben Bernanke took every opportunity to talk down the potential bubble forming during the mid-2000s. The economy was recovering strongly from a series of blows early in the decade, which began with the technology bubble bursting, followed by the 9/11 terrorist attacks, and culminating with a series of corporate accounting scandals. The good old days were back thanks to the sustained low level of interest rates Chairman Greenspan had put in place to counter these negative events. Strong economic growth supported one of the legs of the Federal Reserve's dual mandate—full employment. Figure 6.9 highlights that until the other leg of the mandate—inflation—was about to breach policy makers' comfort zone of 2 percent they would do nothing to reign in a credit bubble in the making.

Even as the bubble grew, central bankers minimized the implications of an overheating housing market. Chairman Bernanke dismissed the idea that housing prices could even decline on a nationwide basis. Figure 6.10 highlights some of the current and former Fed Chairmen's ill-timed quotes. Former Chairman Greenspan spoke up in 2006 to say that the bursting of a bubble is really no big deal judging from the minimal impact that the end of the tech bubble had on the economy. Chairman Bernanke remained behind the curve as late as January 2008 saying that no full-blown recession was anticipated by the Federal Reserve. According to the National Bureau of Economic Research Business

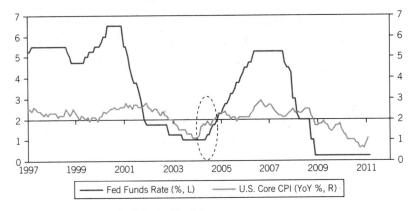

Figure 6.9   Fed Adheres to Its Inflation Mandate
Source: Wolfe Trahan & Co.

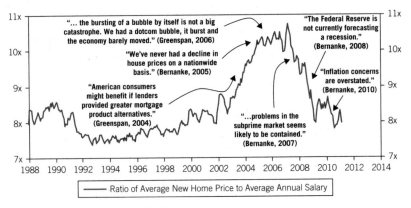

Figure 6.10   The Fed Is Reactive, Not Proactive
Source: Wolfe Trahan & Co.

Cycle Dating Committee—which Ben Bernanke sat on prior to his tenure at the Fed—the recession had actually started a full year prior to that statement.[8]

Chapter Summary

- There are two ways to think about the massive failure to antic-ipate the housing and credit debacle by Wall Street banks: either they didn't understand the risk exposure their firms had to highly risky assets, or they did understand but failed to act. This has led to a new era of uncertainty and a lack of trust in the financial industry.

- Working day to day in the weeds of the financial markets can cloud judgment, similar to the Fog of War. Using historical macro trends as a guide can help maintain perspective, avoid complacency, and prevent extreme extrapolation from current conditions.

- Investors not too deep in the weeds could see that the housing bubble was predictable. Similar to past bubbles, ample access to credit drove its inflation and an accommodative Federal Reserve led to a massive expansion of credit. Telltale signs included: media frenzy, stretched valuations, signs of speculation, breadth of participation, and an imbalance between supply and demand.

- Bubbles are serial in nature; trends in monetary policy dovetail with the creation and destruction of bubbles during the last several decades.

PART

III

CURRENT POLICIES ARE LEADING US DOWN AN UNSUSTAINABLE PATH

The lifecycle of the housing bubble may have been fairly typical for a credit-induced mania, but the aftermath of the ensuing recession has been an unfamiliar experience for the United States. The last several economic downturns were addressed with easy monetary policy to restart credit creation and job growth, and before long the country was on its way to creating the next asset bubble. This time, more than two years after the end of the latest recession, neither demand for credit nor employment is anywhere close to levels seen before the bubble burst.

Policy makers have continued on the familiar course of easing monetary conditions, but gained little traction because they are not considering the new position of the United States in the global economy. The emerging economies are driving global economic growth, while the American consumer is trying to *reduce*, not increase, consumption and debt levels. Instead of boosting the domestic consumer sector, ultra-easy monetary policy has largely been exported to fuel the growth of our trading partners. Years of deficit spending, even during periods of prosperity, have left the United States in a fiscal hole as well. The politics of short-term gain for long-term pain have put the country on an unsustainable path, and some very difficult sacrifices will be required to reverse course.

No More Tools in the Toolbox

No policy can be considered sound which does not take into account all groups which are affected, and what the effect of that policy will be in the long term.[1]

—Henry Hazlitt

The Federal government threw the largest dose of stimulus in decades at the economy to pull it out of the 2007 to 2008 recession. Many temporary, targeted programs like Cash for Clunkers and the first-time homebuyer's tax credit included in the stimulus package have come and gone, but there are also aggressive, broad policy moves still in play. The White House and Congress have given Americans a more than $800 million fiscal shot in the arm in the form of tax breaks, and the Federal Reserve has maintained a prolonged zero-interest-rate policy after a decline of 500 basis points in the federal funds rate.

With the policy rate already as low as it could go, the Fed then continued on the course to pump liquidity into the system by embarking on several rounds of quantitative easing—purchasing Treasury securities to boost the money supply. Quantitative easing effectively suppressed interest rates further, which encouraged investors to move capital from low-yielding bonds and cash toward riskier assets like equities. The equity market took its cue beautifully and rallied significantly. Low interest rates in the United States relative to other countries caused outflows from lower-yielding, dollar-denominated assets, which put downward pressure on the dollar. The Fed was using the dollar as a "policy tool of last resort."

A depressed currency was the final variable available to manipulate the flow of capital toward riskier assets like equities, and away from the safe haven of cash. There are far reaching consequences of this policy, however, and they are being felt around the globe. The weaker dollar successfully boosted stock prices, as shown in Figure 7.1, but it also resulted in higher commodity prices, which in turn threatened global growth. The macro trend of our depressed currency has been one of the most important influences on markets around the world in the last several years: The negative correlation between the dollar and domestic equities has been extremely tight. It appears that by embarking on not one but two rounds of quantitative easing, the Fed thought there really *was* a free lunch, or at least a lunch that could be paid for with a depreciated dollar. In the end the Fed will find that the meal wasn't free, and the bill is due with massive interest.

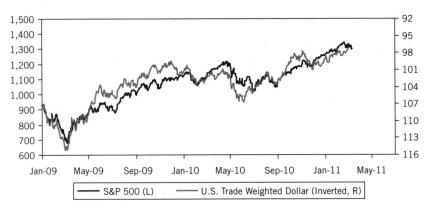

Figure 7.1   The Heightened Role of the Dollar
Source: Wolfe Trahan & Co.

Despite the overwhelming stimulus injected into the economy, the post-recession recovery has been one of the weakest of the past 50 years. Employment has been particularly resistant to improvement, as shown in Figure 7.2. In fact, the latest post-recessionary period suffers under the most anemic job-recovery rate since World War II. The Federal Reserve has run out of conventional policy

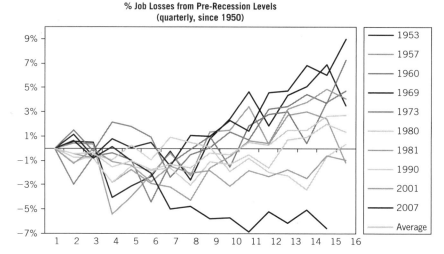

Figure 7.2   Weakest Employment Recovery in More Than 50 Years
Source: Wolfe Trahan & Co.

tools, but a very important sector of the economy still has a long way to go to reach even pre-recession levels.

Companies' reluctance to hire has thrown a wrench into the Fed's strategy to exit the easy-policy environment. One part of the central bank's mandate is to maintain price stability, and the longer stimulative policy remains in place, the greater the likelihood inflation will take root. Another part of the Fed's mandate, however, is to promote full employment. These two goals are now at odds, and juggling them is particularly difficult in a world where the Fed no longer dominates global monetary policy.

A Breakdown in the Traditional Economic Model of the United States

The biggest headwind to an economic renewal has been consumer deleveraging. Despite the prolonged period of near-zero interest rates, spending did not bounce back like previous recoveries. Consumers did not demand credit, as they had in the past, instead choosing to pay down debt accumulated during years of credit-fueled spending. Meanwhile, hiring and wages did not recover sufficiently to enable consumers to fill the resulting spending gap.

Debt elimination is positive for the longer-term health of household balance sheets, but consumer austerity is dealing a severe blow to recovery in the short term. Deleveraging has also changed the way relationships between economic variables evolve. Historically, saving became less attractive in a low rate environment since the interest paid out was reduced. During this recovery, the savings rate actually *increased* despite interest rates hovering near historical lows. Figure 7.3 shows how the relationship between bond yields and the savings rate has changed in recent years.

Figure 7.3   Lower Rates No Longer Automatically Lead to Lower Savings
Source: Wolfe Trahan & Co.

During the Greenspan era at the Fed, all the central bank had to do to stimulate growth and credit was cut interest rates. Chairman Greenspan was able to avoid allowing the business cycle to move into recessionary territory by juicing up growth with additional liquidity before the contraction worsened. Americans took the bait and spent their way into a new phase of prosperity, at least until this never-ending cycle of liquidity overheated. The Federal Reserve is finding that pulling the familiar levers of monetary policy now produces very different results. The hair of the dog—low interest rates—could not prompt consumers to once again get drunk on credit. This sea change in consumer behavior caught policy makers and economists unprepared. Most economic models were not built with deleveraging in mind—just as many mortgage-backed-securities models used on Wall Street did not consider that housing prices could ever fall. The environment now calls for a very different set of assumptions and policy tools. Every economic forecast from this point onward should embed the new reality that there is now less leverage available to enhance growth.

The shift in psychology toward deleveraging fundamentally transformed Americans' relationship with credit and debt. Much has been made of the reduced supply of credit due to tighter bank lending standards during the recession, but the other side of the coin is that consumers were, and are, *demanding* less credit as well. The results of a study by the Experian credit agency, illustrated in Figure 7.4, showed that American consumers were opening 26 percent fewer credit cards than they had been just three years prior. Many people have switched to pay-as-you-go debit cards instead of racking up more credit card debt. This represents quite a shift from

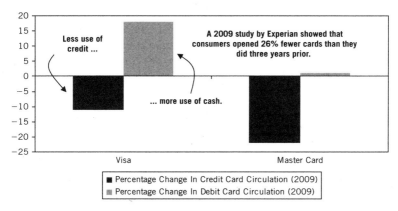

Figure 7.4   Consumers Are Moving Away from Credit Cards
Source: Wolfe Trahan & Co.

the credit-happy years of the early 2000s. Without leveraging their incomes, Americans' spending abilities are limited, which greatly changes how consumers affect the growth equation.

It's All About the Consumer!

The American economic story begins and ends with the consumer: This sector is responsible for more than 70 percent of economic output, as represented by the "C" in the equation in Figure 7.5. Accounting for more than two thirds of growth means that the consumer is the most important driver of a recovery—or a downturn,

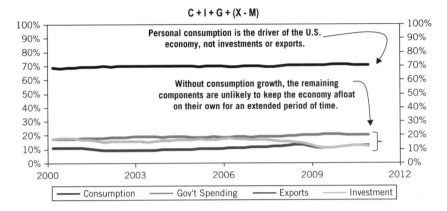

Figure 7.5   The American Economy Has a Huge Concentration Risk . . . the Consumer
Note: In the GDP equation, C stands for consumption, I for investment, G for government spending, X for exports, and M for imports.
Source: Wolfe Trahan & Co.

as we recently witnessed. Trade, investment and government spending factor into the equation as well, but it's unlikely these sectors can keep the economy afloat when they each comprise 20 percent or less of gross domestic product. The difficulty of reviving spending while consumers are deleveraging has prompted the Federal government to prop up these other components of GDP, but without lasting success. Government spending certainly was a bandage during the last several years, but both the likelihood and effectiveness of further government stimulus measures are doubtful despite that the wound is not fully healed. Reviving employment and consumer spending are likely the best way to achieve a sustainable recovery, but there are no easy answers for how to accomplish this goal.

With traditional measures of stimulus already exhausted, factors that would normally be less influential, such as the dollar or mild inflation, have become a primary concern. Even small movements in these variables become more important when a major policy tool like the federal funds rate has been neutralized. Policy makers have embraced the dollar as the only tool left to manipulate since interest rates are already near zero, and accordingly the Federal government has made it the cornerstone of a plan to boost the United States economy through foreign trade. In President Obama's 2010 State of the Union Address he called for a doubling of exports by 2015. With this announcement, the National Exports Initiative (NEI) was formed to help farmers and medium and small businesses, the engines of American growth, increase their exposure to the 95 percent of the world's customers that live outside the United States. While doubling exports seems like an aggressive goal, it has happened before. Since 1970, the United States has accomplished this feat in a five-year period several times. Notably, each one of these episodes coincided with a steep multi-year drop in the value of the dollar. Although the resulting sharp rise in exports would seem to boost the economy, the benefits only last for a short period. A weaker dollar makes American goods more attractive for export, but the trade sector's stimulus is the consumer's burden! A declining dollar hurts consumers because as the currency weakens, the cost of goods imported into the United States rises. Higher import prices eventually flow through the supply chain from producers to consumers, especially when corporate margins are under pressure and companies are forced to raise the price of their goods. The chart in Figure 7.6 shows that an export boom fueled by a weaker dollar is almost always followed by recession.

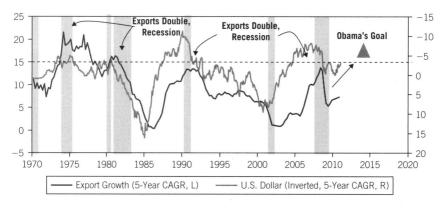

Figure 7.6   Export-Driven Policies Could Send the United States Back Into a Recession
Note: Shaded areas indicate periods of recession.
Source: Wolfe Trahan & Co.

The strategy often appears to work at first, with exports booming and the trade deficit improving, but the hangover always arrives. During the export booms in 1973, 1979, 1992, and 2007, headlines touted the economic benefits of the falling trade deficit, but the good news did not last for long. The story changed, sometimes within a matter of months, and then the news became focused on soaring inflation and the possibility (or reality) of recession. Figure 7.7 shows some of the boom and bust headlines from past dollar-driven export booms.

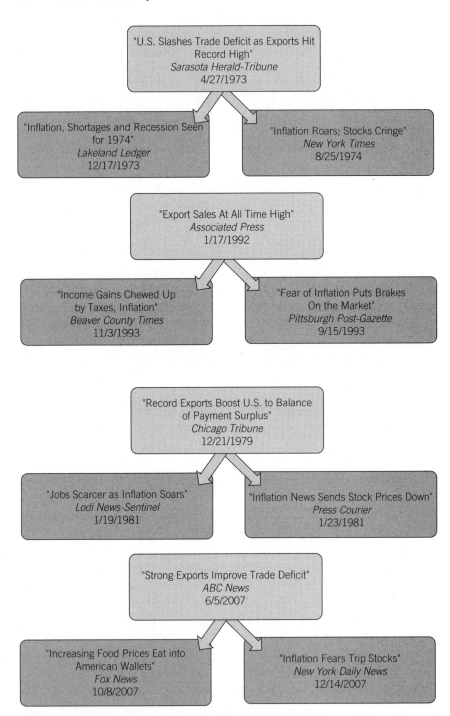

Figure 7.7   Headlines from Past Export Booms and Inflation Busts
Source: Wolfe Trahan & Co.

The Administration's logic is that a weaker dollar makes American goods cheaper in the global marketplace, and, therefore, more attractive than higher-priced competitors' products. Increasing our exports could, in theory, add to GDP and create more jobs that support the manufacturing of goods in the United States. This plan fails, though, because unlike export-heavy economies such as China or South Korea, the United States cannot devalue its way to prosperity and competitiveness. *The United States has the largest gap in the world in the amount of growth contributed to GDP by consumption over exports.* This is one list that Americans should not want to lead.

Exports Are Not Enough

Exports as a percentage of the United States economy have been on the rise since the end of World War II, but still only account for 12 percent of GDP. Meanwhile, consumption accounts for 71 percent, leaving a massive 59 percent gap between the two. As Figure 7.8 illustrates, this gap puts the United States amongst the countries *least* likely to benefit from an export boom. Even from a job creation perspective, the impact of increasing exports is minimal. Employment in the United States tied to exporting of goods and services accounts for only nine million jobs, or about 7 percent of total employment.[2] Pumping up such a small segment of the economy can have only a marginal effect—not nearly enough to promote a sustainable recovery.

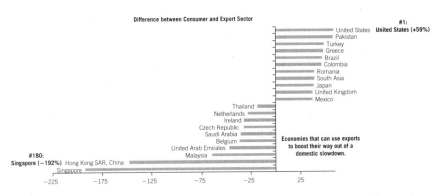

Figure 7.8   The United States Has the Largest Differential Between Consumption and Exports in the World

Source: Wolfe Trahan & Co.

Pursuing a pro-trade, weaker dollar policy is not only ineffective for driving growth, but could actually damage the economy. A weaker dollar makes our goods cheaper for other nations to buy, but it also makes goods imported into the country more expensive. Everything from food to gas to clothing and toys costs more for Americans when buying them with a weaker dollar. The big question for the United States is, *at what point does currency weakness hurt consumers more than it helps exporters?* That point is much closer for the United States than it is for a nation like China where household spending and exports are more balanced. The last time we saw the impact of a weak dollar was in 2007 when the Federal Reserve was lowering interest rates and other countries were tightening. This led to a 10 percent drop in the dollar and a subsequent pickup in exports, but rising commodity prices and inflation were the byproducts. Once the price of oil leapt over $95 per barrel, it acted as a tax on consumers and took a bite out of spending. The GDP boost generated from exporting our goods did not come close to outweighing the burden Americans felt when gas spiked north of $4 per gallon at the pump. The moral of the story is that beyond the very short run, currency depreciation hurts more than it helps in countries highly dependent on household consumption, especially when many of the goods they consume are imported.

The weak dollar engineered by the Fed's quantitative easing in 2009 and 2010 again produced a temporary enhancement to growth, just as it did in 2007. As the fiscal crisis in Greece eased in mid-2010, the Euro rebounded and the dollar fell by 15 percent helping to boost both exports from the United States and asset prices globally. Stronger exports were behind much of the rebound in domestic economic activity in the second half of 2010. The dollar filled its magnified role of growth stimulant very well, but global central bankers play a game of chicken with inflation by maintaining this policy. While the Fed tries to sustain low interest rates and spark growth, the rest of the world is taming inflation by raising rates, or at least keeping them constant. This is quite a different story from late 2008 and early 2009 when central banks around the world were easing policy. At that time, the American currency was strong as investors bid up "safety assets" such as the dollar and Treasurys. Everything changed when leading indicators around the world

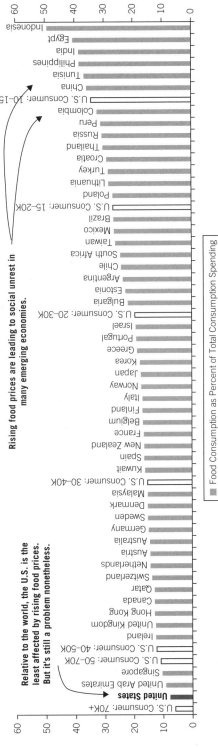

Figure 7.9   Rising Food Prices Are a Big Problem in Emerging Economies

Source: Wolfe Trahan & Co.

91

began to recover. In that scenario, the harder Chairman Bernanke presses on the quantitative easing pedal, the more other central bankers in high-growth countries like China, Brazil, India, and Korea need to raise their rates to contain prices. Rising commodity prices, especially in food-related raw inputs, take an enormous bite out of the household budget in an emerging economy. Data in Figure 7.9 show that in the United States, a typical American family spends roughly 10 percent of its budget on food, but in emerging countries the food budget can demand upward of 30 to 50 percent of income. It's hardly a surprise that central bankers in these emerging countries are aggressive about stamping out inflation given the impact it has on their people.

As basic costs go up, workers begin demanding higher wages to compensate for the higher cost of living, which in turn makes the goods they produce more expensive. In today's globalized world, those upward pricing pressures ultimately filter through to the American consumer in the form of higher import prices. Higher prices for food, energy, and other goods then take a greater bite out of American consumers' disposable incomes, which undermines the effects of easy policy.

The bottom line is that there is no trade-related, weak-dollar shortcut around the American consumer playing a starring role in a sustainable economic recovery. Figure 7.10 illustrates that consumption and exports are far from interchangeable. The greatest challenge of this cycle is that both pillars that traditionally propped up the powerful consumer—credit and employment income—are damaged. Under the new and unfamiliar paradigm of consumer deleveraging, the importance of jobs and wage growth are enhanced in the consumer spending equation. Prior to the financial crisis, consumers relied on credit and liquidity engendered by Fed rate cuts and rising home prices to fuel spending when wage growth was not enough. With the policy rate bound at zero and credit

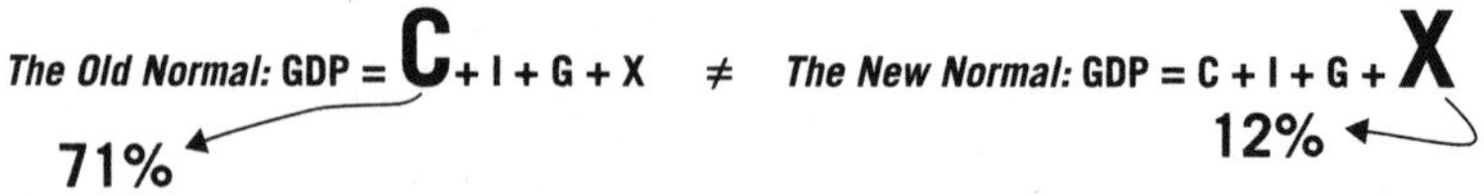

$$\textit{The Old Normal: GDP} = \mathbf{C} + I + G + X \quad \neq \quad \textit{The New Normal: GDP} = C + I + G + \mathbf{X}$$

71%   12%

Figure 7.10   The Old Normal Does Not Equal the New Normal for GDP
Source: Wolfe Trahan & Co.

still either unavailable or undesirable, this is no longer the case. Deleveraging is forcing a movement away from credit, not toward it, and the job market has not snapped back to even its pre-recession levels. An employment recovery strong enough to actually take up the slack that credit has left is still many years away. In the mean time, a weak dollar only exacerbates the strains on the stretched consumer balance sheet.

Chapter Summary

- The White House and Congress have given Americans an $800+ million fiscal shot in the arm in the form of tax breaks, and the Federal Reserve has maintained a prolonged zero-interest-rate policy. Under these conditions, the dollar became the "policy tool of last resort." The Fed embarked on several rounds of quantitative easing to suppress interest rates further, which drove the dollar much lower.
- The biggest headwind to the economic recovery has been consumer deleveraging. Deleveraging has caused a breakdown in the traditional economic model in the United States.
- Attempts to boost exports are not only insufficient, but potentially harmful. *The United States has the largest gap in the world in the amount of growth contributed to GDP by consumption over exports.* Unlike export-heavy economies, the United States cannot devalue its way to prosperity and competitiveness.
- A weaker dollar makes American goods more attractive for export, but the trade sector's stimulus is the consumer's burden! A declining dollar hurts consumers because as the currency weakens, the cost of goods imported into the United States rises. Higher import prices eventually flow through the supply chain from producers to consumers, especially when corporate margins are under pressure and companies are forced to raise the price of their goods. An export boom fueled by a weaker dollar is almost always followed by recession.

8

The Government's Un-Safety Net

Pull the string, and it will follow wherever you wish. Push it, and it will go nowhere at all.[1]

—Dwight Eisenhower

W hen Congress created the United States Federal Reserve System nearly a hundred years ago the main purpose was to maintain the safety and stability of the nation's monetary and financial systems.[2] Over the years, the Fed's responsibilities have grown. In the late 1970s, the Fed's mandate was changed to incorporate the pursuit of maximum employment while maintaining price stability and moderate long-term interest rates.[3]

Recently, the paths toward full employment and price stability have been at odds. As employment has remained stubbornly weak, it seems like the Fed is choosing to target higher equity prices to support the economic recovery, and putting price stability concerns on the back burner. The results of sustained ultra-easy policy via a weak dollar and artificially suppressed interest rates may give the Fed no choice but to again put inflation concerns front and center.

The stimulus thrown at the economy in the wake of the housing crisis created the largest government safety net this country has seen since the Great Depression. Since 2008, more than half of the increase in personal spending can be attributed to government transfer payments and lower taxes. Figure 8.1 shows how personal income, not including government aid, and consumer spending patterns diverged since the beginning of the stimulus programs.

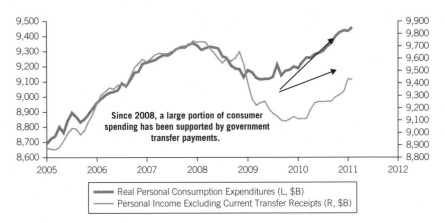

Figure 8.1   The Government Has Kept the Consumer Afloat
Source: Wolfe Trahan & Co.

Data on the consumer, taken at face value, appear to be improving, but so far the government training wheels have been largely responsible for keeping the recovery on track.

More than a year after the recession officially ended,[4] neither employment nor core inflation had trended back up to the Fed's comfort zone. The economic stagnation led to a severe drop in the Taylor Rule,[5] a formula that Fed economists rely upon to help them understand whether monetary policy should be looser or tighter. This drop encouraged the Fed to continue successive cuts in the policy rate. Given policy makers' reliance on the Taylor Rule, it comes as no surprise that the Fed has been unwilling to back away from its stimulus efforts. The absence of inflationary pressures made room for the Fed to try to boost growth by extending its quantitative easing (QE) program into a second round, and lowering the effective policy rate well into negative territory. Prior to the round of QE begun in November 2010, New York Federal Reserve Bank President William Dudley estimated that the impact of the second installment of QE would bring the effective policy rate down to "only" –3.4 percent by the second half of 2011, while the Taylor Rule called for a policy rate of –7 percent! Those are incredible numbers! The Fed's own model was telling it that the environment warranted a federal funds rate that was not just negative, but extraordinarily negative. Those calculations implied that a Federal funds rate decline of more than 12 percentage points from its peak in the third quarter of 2007 was necessary. At the time, this discrepancy communicated to the Fed that there was room for even more growth in the money supply.

Inflation Enters the Picture

Anyone who does the shopping for a typical American household probably would have disagreed with the Fed's belief that inflation was declining in late 2010 when the second round of QE was launched. It's important to understand what the Fed means when it talks about inflation. Policy makers are focused on *core consumer prices*, a measure of inflation that excludes historically volatile food and energy prices. The reasoning behind this is that the prices of food and energy can experience large swings propelled by factors outside the influence of the economic cycle. These factors could include weather patterns disrupting crop supplies, or the Organization of the Petroleum Exporting Countries (OPEC) setting output constraints on oil. Price fluctuations due to these types of events do not require a policy response, and so the Fed opts to strip out their effects when evaluating the stability of prices.

When the Fed eases policy rates to stimulate the economy out of a recession, one of its goals is to bring the annual growth rate in core prices back up to an informal target of around 2 percent per year. In the past this was accomplished by lowering interest rates to pump liquidity into the system, which encouraged lending and stimulated consumer demand. The rules of the game have changed, however, and accomplishing these goals during a deleveraging cycle is more challenging. In response to the Fed's near-zero interest rates, consumers increased their savings instead of their spending, and lending standards remained high as banks worked off bad loans from their books. Rates languished at rock-bottom levels with little consumer response, and the threat of deflation concerned the Fed more than inflation. As a last resort, the central bank ventured into two rounds of quantitative easing. QE effectively lowered the implied policy rate and sparked higher prices, but not exactly in the way the Fed would have preferred. Driving down interest rates suppressed the dollar and encouraged equities to rally as taking on portfolio risk became "cheaper." At the same time, the weaker dollar contributed to driving up the prices of commodities globally. Inflation in food and energy was picking up around the world, but the core price level in the United States drifted lower. These circumstances left the Fed in the unfamiliar position of trying to stimulate the consumer sector—keeping rates low—while the rest of the world was fighting inflation—raising rates. The rate differential only served to reinforce dollar weakness as capital flowed toward higher-yielding assets in other countries. Figure 8.2 shows how the policy rate in the United States diverged from that of other countries in 2010, and that in turn depressed the dollar. The Fed played the same cards that it always had played, but the game turned out differently. Why was it so different this time around?

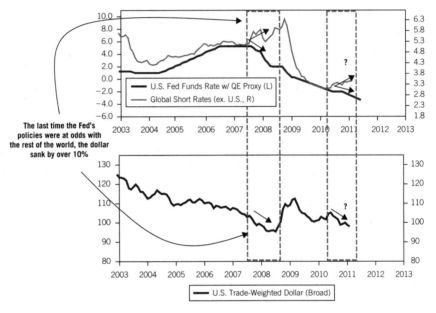

Figure 8.2   Central Bank Policy Weighing on the Dollar
Source: Wolfe Trahan & Co.

Spinning Our Wheels

For many decades, the United States was the sole price setter for commodities. During the 1980s and 1990s, commodity price fluctuations helped support policy moves by the Federal Reserve. When the American economy was red hot, higher commodity prices helped reinforce tightening measures that the central bank was enacting: Higher interest rates and higher commodity prices both served to dampen growth. The inverse was true when the economy cooled: Lower rates increased liquidity and lower food and energy prices demanded a smaller chunk of consumers' disposable income. This dynamic changed about 10 years ago, as shown in Figure 8.3, and the new world order is likely here to stay. Going forward, the Fed will have no choice but to change the way it looks at how its policy impacts the rest of the world.

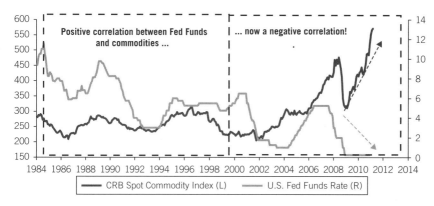

Figure 8.3   The Fed Has Exported Easy Policy Around the World and Lifted Commodity Prices
Source: Wolfe Trahan & Co.

In essence, the United States exports its policy to all of the countries pegged to the dollar. China benefitted early on from our easy monetary policy without the drag the United States experienced from the unwinding of its credit excesses. China grew out of the global recession quickly, while America languished. The weak dollar helped drive rising commodity prices, but this time the rise was out of synch with economic growth in the United States. As food and energy prices rose globally, the impact on the domestic economy became one in which the Fed was trying to ease but was *de facto* tightening instead.

Unlike wage-driven inflation, commodity price inflation can severely cut into disposable income because there is no compensating upward income adjustment in the latter case. Given the high proportion of income spent on food in emerging countries, unchecked prices quickly instigate unrest. Prior to the recession in 2008, food riots erupted in many countries as the cost of staples like rice and wheat skyrocketed. In early 2011, food inflation and meager economic opportunities contributed to the revolutions that erupted in the Middle East and North Africa. The Fed doesn't want to be seen as the cause of this inflationary spiral and, amazingly, Chairman Bernanke has repeatedly denied that his policies contributed to commodity inflation. Despite the incredibly strong relationship between money supply and commodity prices shown in Figure 8.4, Mr. Bernanke puts the blame on demand from emerging markets:

> I think it's entirely unfair to attribute excess demand pressures in emerging markets to U.S. monetary policy, because emerging markets have all the tools they need to address excess demand in those countries. It's really up to emerging markets to find appropriate tools to balance their own growth.
>
> *Comments by Federal Reserve Chairman Ben Bernanke,*
> *National Press Club, Washington, D.C., February 3, 2011*

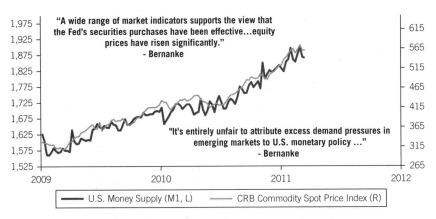

Figure 8.4   Food Prices Have Risen in Lockstep with U.S. Money Supply Growth
Source: Wolfe Trahan & Co.

At the same time, Mr. Bernanke is more than willing to claim responsibility for the role of quantitative easing in boosting equity prices:

> A wide range of market indicators supports the view that the Federal Reserve's securities purchases have been effective at easing financial conditions.
>
> *Comments by Federal Reserve Chairman Ben Bernanke,*
> *National Press Club, Washington, D.C., February 3, 2011*

Without a doubt, the unintended consequences of quantitative easing have manifested in inflationary pressures in the East, and they are moving quickly to the West, as illustrated in Figure 8.5. Leading indicators in China were showing pressure in early 2011 as the country's central bank had already been in policy-tightening mode for over a year. Inflation was red hot in that emerging powerhouse, fueled by rising food prices which make up about a third of China's inflation gauge. Even fiscally plagued Europe was beginning to feel the pressures through import prices, particularly in Germany, the region's economic engine. Both the European Central Bank and the Bank of England were close behind in declaring their discomfort with mounting inflation pressures and signaling a tightening bias. American policy makers, accustomed to calling the global shots, are in for a rude awakening. Despite the lackluster domestic economy, pricing pressures from halfway around the world will boost inflation regardless of the Fed's intentions.

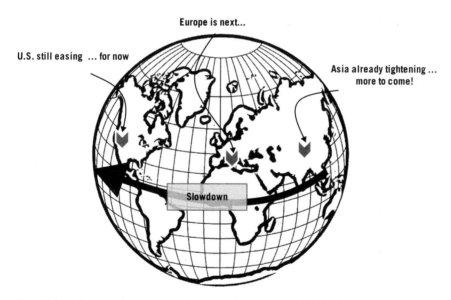

Figure 8.5   Inflation and Policy Tightening to Slow Growth from East to West
Source: Wolfe Trahan & Co.

Nowhere Fast

Some analysts have compared America's ultra-easy monetary policy to that of Japan during the Lost Decade of the 1990s. In some ways the comparison is justified, but in several others it is not. The nature of the policies and the speed of implementation differed greatly in the two cases. The results, however, have been similar.

In both cases, exceptionally low interest rates led to cheap credit, which in turn enabled speculation in land and equities. In Japan, the party ended with more of a slow hiss than a pop. The Finance Ministry raised interest rates to dampen speculation in late 1989, but the decline was long and slow. The equity market fell 63 percent during the following decade and troubled banks had to wait years before being bailed out by the government. Unlike most Americans' experience, the impact on the daily life of the average Japanese person was small. Japanese corporations were in terrible shape, but the individual fared much better due to the cultural tendency toward frugality and high savings rates. The Japanese responded extremely slowly in addressing the problems. The initial reaction was to do nothing as banks faltered, and by the time the government injected public funds into the economy it had been over a decade since the onset of the malaise. It took the Bank of Japan nearly a year and a half to cut interest rates, and 10 years for them to reach zero. Inflation has languished near zero ever since.

In contrast, the United States moved quickly. Interest rates were cut with lightning speed and a bailout package quickly emerged for the banks. Perhaps the Federal Reserve drew on the lessons of Japan to act more quickly, but they are doing essentially the same things. Both American and Japanese policy responses have suffered from shortsightedness. During their slow economic decline, Japanese leaders failed to grasp the severity and depth of the crisis they faced. They made attempts to fix the economy in the short run, but did nothing to address the longer term, structural problems. The same goes for the United States. Take, for example, the payroll tax holiday bundled with the extension of the Bush tax cuts at the end of 2010. This was, in a sense, akin to the infamous helicopter drop of cash instituted by the Japanese. Cash for clunkers and the first time home buyers tax credit fall into the same category of bridges half built. And yet, Chairman Bernanke seems perplexed that American consumers have not yet reassumed their role as the primary engine of economic growth. Consumer action has not supported recovery because the underlying problems have not been addressed, and because Fed policy responses have been unproductive, and in some cases even counter-productive.

In fact, the United States is much more vulnerable than Japan in several ways. Most Japanese bonds are owned by the Japanese, unlike the United States, which has more than half of its Treasurys held by foreign creditors.[6] This makes us more vulnerable on the currency front, and thus much more vulnerable to inflation, as well. Chairman Bernanke seems to believe that if he can somehow create inflation it will be good for the economy: If we have inflation we will not be Japan. He has indeed created inflation, but in income-sapping food and energy prices instead of wage gains for workers.

The tragic earthquake and resulting tsunami that hit Japan in March 2011 showed what can happen when a country has no economic margin of error. When a country is plagued with deficits—Japan was estimated to have a public debt-to-GDP ratio of 225 percent in 2010, second only to Zimbabwe[7]—an unforeseen tragedy can burden the government with additional debts it cannot pay. Unfortunately, if something similar happened in the United States we would likely be in a comparable position. Until we address the underlying issues that brought us to the current impasse, policy makers simply are putting a bandage on gangrene. We, too, are kicking the can down the road.

Chapter Summary

- Recently, the paths toward full employment and price stability have been at odds. As employment has remained stubbornly weak, it seems like the Fed is choosing to target higher equity prices to support the economic recovery, and putting price stability concerns on the back burner.
- When the Fed talks about inflation it means core inflation, which excludes historically volatile food and energy prices. The reasoning behind this is that the prices of food and energy can experience large swings propelled by factors outside the influence of the economic cycle.
- In response to the Fed's near-zero interest rates consumers increased their savings instead of their spending, and lending standards remained high as banks worked off bad loans from their books.
- During the 1980s and 1990s, the United States was the sole price setter for commodities. This dynamic changed about 10 years ago, and the new world order is likely here to stay. Going forward, the Fed will have no choice but to change the way it looks at how its policy impacts the rest of the world.

CHAPTER

Kicking the Can Down the Road

The best way to destroy the capitalist system is to debauch the currency. By a continuing process of inflation, governments can confiscate, secretly and unobserved, an important part of the wealth of their citizens.[1]

—John Maynard Keynes

Wouldn't it be nice if everybody had the same definition of compromise as the U.S. government? Everyone would literally be better off. Compromise generally means giving up something to get an acceptable measure of what you want, but the government's definition is somewhat different: It means getting what you want by also letting the other guy get what he wants. This type of free-lunch compromise is at the core of Washington, D.C.'s proclivity for kicking the can on longer-term problems. At some point in the near future, however, the "longer term" will come crashing into the present.

QE Was an Experiment

If Fed officials were honest about it, they would admit the second round of quantitative easing (QE2) was an experiment. Maybe unconventional policies were warranted after tried and true interest rate cuts barely moved the needle, but the longer-run implications will be unclear for some time. The fictitious tombstone ad in Figure 9.1 is an attempt to convey a financial market comparison to QE2. Essentially, the second round of easing was equivalent to an equity offering made by a company that can no longer issue debt obligations—or in the Fed's case, can no longer lower interest rates conventionally. This is probably not the type of company an investor would want to own!

This announcement is neither an offer to sell nor a solicitation of an offer to buy any of these Securities and is *100% fake*.

November 3, 2010

500 Billion Dollars of
United States Currency

With over 300 million people and more than 3.79 million square miles, the United States is the third largest country by both population and land area.

The Board of Governors of The Federal Reserve System acted as Financial Advisor to the U.S. government

Board of Governors of The
Federal Reserve System

20th Street and Constitution Avenue NW, Washington, DC

Figure 9.1   Free Lunch?
Source: Wolfe Trahan & Co.

Unfortunately, Americans do not benefit from this kind of policy in the long run. The short-term advantage may be slightly lower borrowing rates, but in exchange Americans get inflationary pressures in import and commodity prices down the road. Meanwhile, countries with currencies pegged to the dollar get a dose of stimulus in the form of a depreciating currency, and unlike the United States, many of these countries have an export sector large enough to make a significant impact on growth. Eventually, however, they too must address the impact of rising prices. Figure 9.2 shows the affect of the depreciating dollar on the Chinese Yuan. Perhaps the biggest winners are oil-producing countries. They reap massive gains as the price of oil rises on the back of a weaker dollar.

Figure 9.2   Dollar Weakness Spills Over to Much of Emerging Asia
Source: Wolfe Trahan & Co.

Monetary policy has been managed in the last several years as though policy makers were crossing their fingers and hoping the American consumer economy would rebound before the Fed ran out of ammunition. While this rebound has occurred to some degree—with the important exception of employment—the longer-term negative consequences have been building. Global inflationary pressures make further quantitative easing unlikely unless some unforeseen, deflationary event occurs, but the damage has been done. Like a family living on credit cards month to month, the Fed may have finally maxed out its limit.

We're All Keynesians Now . . . Unfortunately?

Monetary policy is not the only way that D.C. has been kicking the can down the road. The government really has taken to heart the famous quote by the economist John Maynard Keynes, "In the long run, we are all dead," in choosing to focus on the short-term benefits of its spending over the long-term costs. Keynesian economic policies have dominated the fiscal response in Washington. In general, Keynesians advocate managing fiscal policy to smooth the ups and downs of the business cycle. The chart in Figure 9.3 is a graphical expression of the Keynesian influence on business cycles, and in particular, government spending patterns. According to Keynes, lowering interest rates was not sufficient to pull an economy out of a severe recession; instead, he supported boosting government spending and tax cuts in order to mitigate periods of sluggish economic growth. In this way, Congress could keep the cyclical lows from getting *too* low. Dampening the upside of the business cycle, however, seems to have been lost on policy makers. Instead of cutting government spending when the economy was booming, they continued to build up deficits.

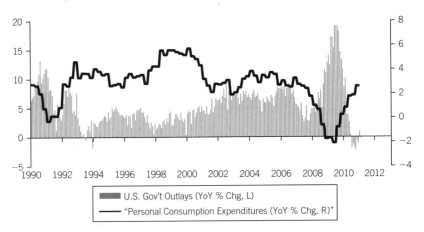

Figure 9.3   As Government Spending Retreats, Consumer Spending Needs to Accelerate
Source: Wolfe Trahan & Co.

The original stimulus bill passed by Congress added about 2 to 2.5 percentage points to GDP in 2009. It is true that without the stimulus funding that level of growth would never have materialized, but unfortunately it amounted to nothing more than a temporary shot in the arm. The bulk of stimulus benefits were reaped in 2009 when the government sector pulled the drag from the consumer above water. By the second half of 2010, the contribution to GDP from fiscal stimulus was set to turn negative. When the time came for the Bush-era tax cuts to expire at the end of 2010, the consumer was judged incapable of shouldering the burden of additional taxes. The political firestorm ended with another Washington compromise: The Republicans obtained tax cut extensions for all income classes through 2012, and the Democrats won additional stimulus in the form of a payroll tax holiday for employees. This short-term fix did nothing to address the real problems facing both the consumer and the government. Essentially, tax payers paid $859B for a fiscal package that only served to push 2011 economic headwinds into 2012, as demonstrated in Figure 9.4, not eliminate them.

The payroll tax holiday was a part of the concessions made by Republicans for Democratic support in extending the Bush-era tax cuts. The payroll tax for employees—a tax that is paid toward Social Security—was cut by about a third, from 6.2 percent to 4.2 percent, in 2011. That amounts to a maximum of $2,136 retained by a worker who earns a salary of $106,800—the top earnings for which the tax applies. For someone who earns the median annual United States income of $50,221[2] the saving boils down to about $84 per month. These are not large numbers, especially for lower-income wage earners who are far more likely to spend the windfall than higher-salaried workers, yet the holiday will cost the government $120 billion in lost revenue.[3] The White House Fact Sheet detailing the fiscal package claims as one of the plan's key accomplishments its focus on high-impact job creation measures:

> *Focused on high impact job creation measures.* The framework agreement includes some of the best measures for jumpstarting growth and job creation, including a full year of emergency unemployment insurance benefits, an about $120 billion payroll tax cut for working families and a continuation of tax credits for working families. This is on top of growth generated by extension of the middle-class income tax rates.
>
> *"Fact Sheet on the Framework Agreement on Middle Class Tax Cuts and Unemployment Insurance,"*
> *Office of the Press Secretary, The White House, December 7, 2010*

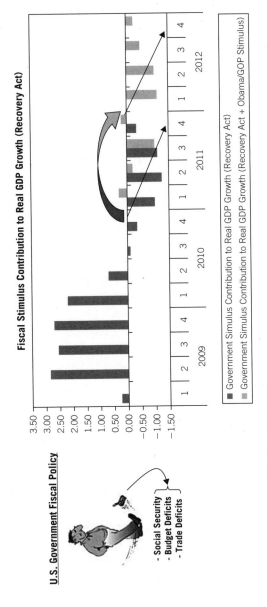

Figure 9.4   Kicking the Can Down the Road
Source: Wolfe Trahan & Co.

It's difficult to see how extending the tax holiday only to employees and not to employers could jumpstart job creation. If the Bush-era tax cuts had been allowed to expire, however, that could have paid for a total elimination of payroll taxes for *employers*, a potent job-creation incentive. When it comes to sacrificing the future for short-term fixes, kicking the can down the road knows no political boundaries.

Uncertainty Kills Growth

If the Federal government really wanted to promote job creation, it would act to reduce uncertainty clouding the future fiscal environment. Given the *structural* nature of the budget gap, most thoughtful people are skeptical that meaningful debt reduction can be accomplished through spending cuts alone. Figure 9.5 shows that even optimistic projections from the Congressional Budget Office leave a structural budget gap. Only $2.2 trillion of the $3.6 trillion fiscal year 2010 budget was financed by Federal tax revenues, with the remaining $1.4 trillion left to be borrowed. The best kept secret in Washington is that taxes will likely need to rise, but nobody will discuss when or by how much. Additional stimulus measures serve to postpone this day of reckoning, which effectively delays businesses' ability to make long-term planning decisions. A sustainable, even if more painful, path toward getting America's fiscal house in order would ease planning for investment and hiring. Uncertainty is kicking real economic growth down the road.

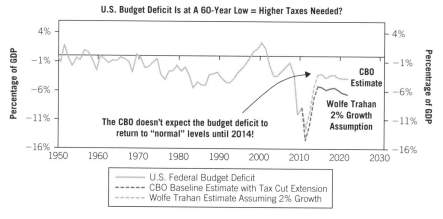

Figure 9.5   U.S. Budget Deficits at 60-Year Low
Source: Wolfe Trahan & Co.

Austerity, in theory, is in fashion in Washington. Despite tough talk about cutting spending, however, proposed cuts have focused on a very small portion of the budget. Figure 9.6 details the spending breakdown in the Obama Administration's 2012 budget proposal. Spending on entitlement programs like Social Security, Medicare, and Medicaid, which make up more than 40 percent of the budget, has scarcely entered the debate, while only small cuts have been proposed to defense spending—another one-fifth of the budget. Democrats have vowed to protect entitlements, and even Republicans have been timid about supporting cuts to these 800 pound gorillas. Proposals to raise the retirement age for Social Security, making benefits more progressive based on income, and placing spending limits on the Medicare and Medicaid programs have all been dismissed on both sides of the aisle. Neither party seems willing to take the steps necessary to put the government on a sustainable path toward balanced revenue and spending.

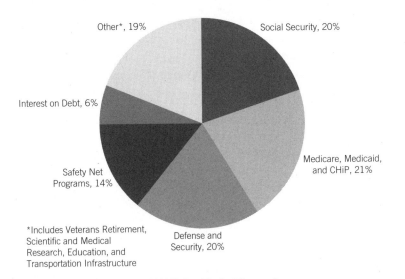

Figure 9.6   Obama Administration's 2012 Federal Budget Proposal

Source: The White House web site, Office of Management and Budget, www.whitehouse.gov/omb/budget

Polls seem to imply that most Americans also believe in Washington-style compromise. As shown in Figure 9.7, most people (77 percent) acknowledge that the Big 3 entitlement programs pose a severe economic challenge, but a majority of Americans also think that neither benefits should be cut (66 percent) nor taxes should be raised (56 percent) to address the problem.[4]

Views on the "major entitlement programs the government is committed to, including Social Security and Medicare"		
	Yes %	No %
Cost of programs will create major economic problems	77	18
Government should raise taxes to address	42	56
Government should cut benefits to address	31	66

Figure 9.7   Views on the Major Entitlement Programs
Source: USA Today/Gallup, Sept. 13–16, 2010

One of the challenges in rallying support for budget sacrifices is that Americans seem to possess severe misconceptions about the composition of the budget. A vast majority think that more is spent on defense and foreign aid than on Medicare and Social Security.[5] Several polls found that Americans are overwhelmingly in favor of cutting foreign aid—which makes up about one percent of the total budget. The only other cuts favored by a majority of people were to the budgets of the Internal Revenue Service and the Securities and Exchange Commission.[6] It's no surprise that politicians of any stripe can get away with citing data that back up his or her position on spending and taxes to a credulous public.

The apparent inconsistencies in these answers could be the result of the way the questions are posed. If the question were framed around making choices between fixing the problems once and for all, or extending the uncertainty, the answers could be quite different. Which option would most individuals choose when faced with the following question?

Would you be more likely to buy a second house under Scenario A or B?

A: Congress passes a fiscal stimulus bill of $2 trillion financed through borrowing

B: The Federal government raises taxes *and* slashes spending to balance the budget

A study in which Americans were given the task of reworking the budget with actual figures and detailed policy tradeoffs produced very different results than the polls discussed earlier. The study, commissioned by Program for Public Consultation,[7] first provided the sample's respondents with information on 31 policy issues and then gave them a range of options for addressing them. While the leaders of the major American political parties largely propose to reduce the deficit by cutting social programs—and doing little or nothing with taxes—average Americans would proceed by cutting defense spending, increasing spending on social programs targeted at higher education and job training, and raising taxes on the wealthy by making them more progressive. In fact, survey respondents proposed about three times more revenue from tax increases than even the Obama administration has budgeted. The end result was far deeper deficit reduction than anything proposed to date by either the Democrats or Republicans.

The differences in priorities between politicians and their constituents could have more to do with income disparity than ideological bias. The median net worth of a Congressperson was more than $900,000 in 2009, while that of the median American family was only $120,000.[8] Perhaps politicians who choose to see the world through the eyes of their constituents, instead of lobbyists and special interest groups, would end up being rewarded at the polls.

Actions speak louder than words, and companies, as well as individuals, are speaking volumes by their lack of investment under the current fiscal dark cloud. Despite strong corporate profit growth, companies have been reluctant to spend cash. Economic uncertainty continues to plague companies' short-term decisions; a better view of the future tax and regulatory environment would enable them to plan with increased certainty. Prolonged haggling over the enforcement of the new financial industry regulations and the health care law clouds the longer-term picture for executives.

The State and Local Time Bomb

The ticking fiscal time bomb of states and municipalities should serve as an example to the Federal government. Potential defaults and widening credit spreads, especially in states that have been less fiscally responsible, have sent shudders through the municipal bond market. Investors have quickly reevaluated a segment of the bond market once regarded as safe and boring. Something similar could potentially happen to Treasury bonds' safe-haven status if the country's fiscal situation is not resolved by making progress toward balanced budgets and restrained borrowing.

Unlike the Federal government, almost every state has some type of formalized balanced budget requirement. These vary from strict, explicit balanced-budget statutes to limitations on state indebtedness, but in most cases traditional practice results in a balanced budget. As a result, many states have had to act aggressively to trim spending after the recession took a bite out of tax revenues. States and local governments have been so hard hit by the implosion of the housing market and the corresponding revenue losses they have had to significantly cut jobs, as shown in Figure 9.8, further worsening the local economic environment.

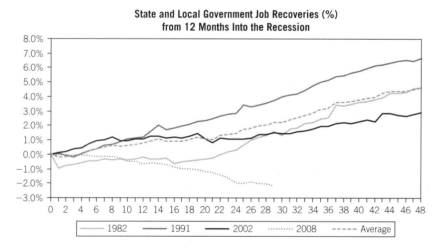

Figure 9.8   Government Jobs Are Declining, Unlike Prior Recessions
Source: Wolfe Trahan & Co.

Bond investors have differentiated, to some degree, between states taking a more fiscally responsible approach and those reluctant to make significant cuts. Figure 9.9 shows that states that have most aggressively shed jobs have enjoyed lower municipal bond yields on average than states that have not. Although both sets experienced rising yields when attention turned toward state budget issues, the differentiation shows that investors are ready to reward austerity over stimulus.

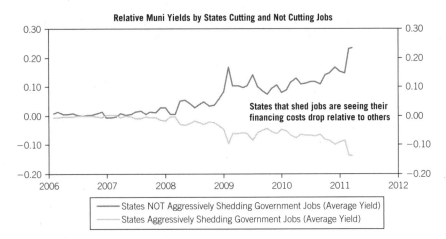

Figure 9.9   Investors Are Punishing States That Are Less Fiscally Responsible
Source: Wolfe Trahan & Co.

Since most states cannot adopt a Keynesian, deficit-spending approach to managing their finances, their "long run" is much closer than that of the Federal government. The states did receive nearly $150 billion from the 2009 American Recovery and Reinvestment Act, but the economic recovery has not been strong enough to bridge the gap since then. Once again, a temporary cash infusion was insufficient to fix the problems and many states are still highly dependent on Federal aid. Only a handful of states are *not* projecting a budget shortfall for fiscal year 2012, yet stimulus funding will largely run out by the end of fiscal 2011. Now, approximately 35 percent of state budgets depend on Federal assistance, up from 25 percent prior to the recession. As the Federal government looks for ways to cut spending while protecting the big entitlement programs, the likelihood of additional aid for states is small.

At some point, the Federal government will have to acknowledge and act to support the types of cuts, and even tax hikes, that the states are currently attempting. For now, policy makers are still working against a real solution. Chairman Bernanke has called for a deficit reduction plan to be phased in over five to 10 years, yet his monetary policy is counteracting that goal. The drag of higher food and energy costs caused by the weak-dollar policy is largely canceling out even short-term benefits of stimulus measures.

The first chart in Figure 9.10 shows that as the effective tax rate falls,[9] as it has during the Obama administration, the amount of disposable income that a consumer has available goes up. The post-recessionary period has seen some of the highest levels of retained disposable income in decades. Since 2008, Americans have gained about 3 additional percentage points of disposable-to-total income. The bottom chart in Figure 9.10, however, tells a different story when it comes to spending. As food and energy prices go up, as they have due to the Fed's weak-dollar policies, those goods eat up a higher percentage of income and leave consumers with *less* room for discretionary spending. *In fact, the extra burden of higher food and energy prices has almost completely erased the disposable income gained from lower taxes in the last several years.* Figure 9.11 details the drain on discretionary spending. If inflationary pressures result in a renewed global slowdown, impactful near-term austerity measures

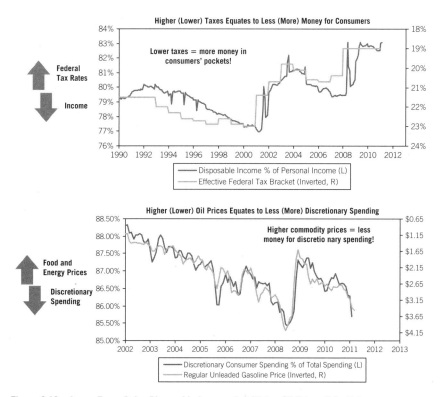

Figure 9.10   Lower Taxes Raise Disposable Income, but Higher Oil Prices Take It Away
Source: Wolfe Trahan & Co.

As a % of Personal Income	2002	2008	2011	2011 Simulation of Gas Prices Gas @ $3.25	Gas @ $3.50	Gas @ $4.00
Income	100.0%	100.0%	100.0%	100.0%	100.0%	100.0%
- Effective Tax Rate	21.0%	19.0%	17.5%	17.5%	17.5%	17.5%
= Disposable Income	79.0%	81.0%	82.5%	82.5%	82.5%	82.5%
- Savings	2.8%	3.2%	4.5%	4.5%	4.5%	4.5%
= Total Spending	76.2%	77.8%	78.0%	78.0%	78.0%	78.0%
- Food and Energy Spending	9.1%	11.3%	10.7%	10.9%	11.1%	11.5%
= Discretionary Spending	67.1%	66.5%	67.2%	67.0%	66.9%	66.4%

Since 2002, rising food and energy prices have offset most of the Bush tax cuts ... leaving the consumer with the same level of dollars available for non-food & energy expenses.

Rising commodity prices eat away at consumers' discretionary dollars.

Figure 9.11   Rising Commodity Prices Are Offsetting Tax Cuts

Source: Wolfe Trahan & Co.

would be far less likely to happen, and could even raise the possibility of additional stimulus. This would put the fiscal situation in the United States on an even more unsustainable path.

The Privatization Option

Depleted budgets and the threat of bankruptcy for some municipalities have forced governments to find creative measures to stay afloat. The 50,000-person city of Maywood, California, has addressed its financial woes by firing all of its workers and outsourcing their jobs.[10] The city's $8 million police department was its biggest drain, taking up more than half of its revenues. Now, Maywood contracts with the Los Angeles County Sheriff's Department at a cost of about half that amount. Many of the town's other municipal workers were hired back on a contract basis, lifting the burden of long-term obligations like pensions.

Privatization of former government functions has become a common topic in the media, and an avenue some politicians are exploring for financial relief. The chart in Figure 9.12, illustrating five-year expected infrastructure investment shortfalls, indicates the severity of the fiscal gap in several critical areas. The hardest hit areas shown in Figure 9.12, like roads and bridges and transport, are the categories in which municipalities and states are most likely to pursue alternative funding options.

Without productive alternatives, budget shortfalls are prompting states to turn back the clock. In an effort to reduce maintenance

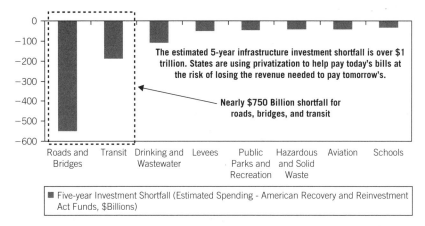

Figure 9.12   Privatization is Likely to Be Seen In Areas with The Largest Budget Shortfalls
Source: Wolfe Trahan & Co.

costs, at least 38 of Michigan's 83 counties have downgraded their roads by pulverizing pavement and leaving gravel in its place. South Dakota has done the same over at least 100 miles of road. North Dakota found it more cost-effective to purchase the $400,000 Caterpillar rotary mixer that grinds up the pavement than to repair the roads in dilapidated condition. This is an attractive option for cash-strapped states since repairing a neglected road has become very expensive. Asphalt cement, one of the major components of blacktop, is a petroleum-based material and has more than doubled in price over the past 10 years.[11]

Despite significant political pushback, it's likely that more and more privatization deals will be implemented as fiscal pressures build. Certain regions have already embraced privatization and many more are considering the possibility. The initiatives shown in Table 9.1 just skim the surface of the scenarios being debated across the country. One of the major benefits of privatization is providing cash up front to fund necessary projects. On the other side of the coin, the opportunity cost involves trading away future revenue streams. Privatization could change the fundamental nature of a broad array of public services, and transform public goods-providing entities into private, for-profit enterprises. The revenues from parking garages, meters, and tunnels could be sold; as well as revenue from care and management of roads,

Table 9.1   Privatization Is Becoming More Commonplace as Budgets Run Dry

Location	Privatization Initiative
Montana	Gov. Brian Schweitzer proposed plans to privatize Medicaid.
Illinois	Former Mayor Richard Daley gave up revenues from 36,000 downtown Chicago parking meters for 75 years in exchange for an upfront payment of $1.15 billion.
California	A city manager proposed to privatize the system that provides water to 10 percent of residents.
Texas	The city council voted unanimously to privatize the Dallas zoo.
Indiana	A city county council voted to sell water and sewer utilities to a charitable trust.
New Jersey	The state began taking bids for private operators to take over highway-toll collection.
Virginia	The governor-proposed plan for the state would sell liquor licenses to generate at least $458 million, according to administration estimates.
Georgia	The Federal Aviation Administration (FAA) accepted the preliminary application by Gwinnett County Airport to participate in the FAA Airport Privatization Program.

Source: Wolfe Trahan & Co

airports, and water and waste systems. Private firms or non-profit trusts might operate zoos, parks, stadiums, and convention centers; and contract for services like accounting, financial, legal, and IT. Notwithstanding the statutory and practical adjustments necessary for such arrangements, they may be the only way to preserve imperiled government functions.

No Short-Term Fixes

The Catch-22 is that cutting spending at any level of government will slow growth in the short run. Cuts to jobs, safety net programs, and spending in general will injure Americans who are already trying to deleverage in the face of higher prices for food and gas. The drag from local governments had shown up in the national data as early as 2010. Larger-than-anticipated cuts by state and local governments were cited in revising the GDP growth rate for Q4 2010 downward. The negative impact comes as no surprise considering the size of the contribution that states make to GDP, as illustrated in Figure 9.13; 60 percent of the government's 21 percent

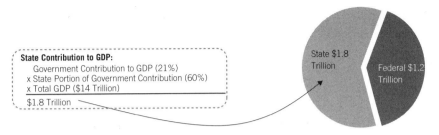

State Contribution to GDP:
Government Contribution to GDP (21%)
x State Portion of Government Contribution (60%)
x Total GDP ($14 Trillion)
_____
$1.8 Trillion

State $1.8 Trillion

Federal $1.2 Trillion

Figure 9.13   Contribution by States to United States GDP
Source: Wolfe Trahan & Co.

share of GDP is attributable to states. That is roughly equivalent to the contribution to GDP made by exports.

Some would argue that the Tea Party movement is a force for change on the fiscal landscape. The group does strongly advocate a balanced budget, but it also endorses immediate tax cuts and indiscriminate spending cuts at any cost. The group's beliefs also favor the present over the future, but are cleverly masked in a fiscally conservative cloak. The real-life budget study discussed earlier in this chapter found that respondents who identified themselves as Tea Party sympathizers actually did the worst job as a group in slashing the deficit.[12] The average net reductions in the deficit, by political party affiliation, are shown in Figure 9.14. Compared

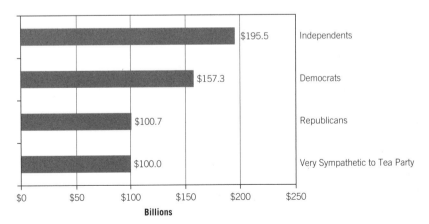

$195.5   Independents

$157.3   Democrats

$100.7   Republicans

$100.0   Very Sympathetic to Tea Party

$0 $50 $100 $150 $200 $250

Billions

Figure 9.14   Average Net Deficit Reduction by Political Party Affiliation
Source: Program for Public Consultation and Knowledge Networks

to Republicans (the next-least-successful deficit cutting group), Democrats, and Independents (the most successful group), Tea Partiers were least likely to raise taxes and, surprisingly, also the least likely to make cuts to spending programs. When asked near the end of the interview session, "How sympathetic are you to the Tea Party movement—very sympathetic, somewhat sympathetic, not very sympathetic, or not at all sympathetic?" 33 percent replied "somewhat sympathetic", and another 14 percent said they were "very sympathetic."

Regardless of the path taken, righting the imbalances at the Federal, state, or local level will probably worsen the employment situation in the near term. Given the anemic level of employment from which we are starting, pushback from the public could become significant. This will likely be one of the biggest discouragements to politicians' and policy makers' efforts to do the right thing. The pushback against some states' attempts to reduce the political power and financial benefits of public sector unionized employees is just the beginning. The longer growth is hampered by ineffective policies and an unstable fiscal situation, however, the more likely that necessary cuts to jobs and spending could turn public sentiment toward protectionism and nationalism. Putting the monetary and fiscal policies of this country on a more sustainable path, although painful in the short run, could actually reduce the tendency toward these economically damaging responses in the long run. Up to this point, though, Washington has not shown that it has the individual and collective backbone to make and implement these difficult choices.

Chapter Summary

- If Fed officials were honest they would admit the second round of quantitative easing was an experiment. The longer-run implications will be unclear for some time.
- Keynesian economic policies have dominated the fiscal response in Washington. Keynesians advocate managing fiscal policy to smooth the ups and downs of the business cycle. Dampening the upside of the business cycle, however, seems to have been lost on policy makers. Instead of cutting government spending when the economy was booming, they continued to build up deficits.

- Given the structural nature of the budget gap, most thoughtful people are skeptical that meaningful debt reduction can be accomplished through spending cuts alone. If the Federal government wanted to promote job creation, it would reduce the uncertainty clouding the future fiscal environment.
- Austerity, in theory, is in fashion in Washington. Despite tough talk about cutting spending, however, proposed cuts have focused on a very small portion of the budget. Spending on entitlement programs and defense, which together make up more than 60 percent of the budget, have barely entered the debate.
- A study in which Americans were given the task of reworking the budget with actual figures and detailed policy tradeoffs produced cuts to defense spending, increases to spending on social programs targeted at higher education and job training, and higher and more progressive taxes. Survey respondents proposed about three times more revenue from tax increases than even the Obama administration has budgeted. The end result was far deeper deficit reduction than anything proposed to date by either the Democrats or Republicans.
- The ticking fiscal time bomb of states and municipalities should serve as an example to the Federal government. States that have most aggressively shed jobs have enjoyed lower municipal bond yields on average than states that have not. The differentiation shows that investors are ready to reward austerity over stimulus.
- The extra burden of higher food and energy prices has almost completely erased the disposable income gained from lower taxes in the last several years.
- There are no short-term fixes. The Catch-22 is that cutting spending at any level of government will slow growth in the short run. Cuts to jobs, safety net programs, and spending in general will injure Americans who are already trying to deleverage in the face of higher prices for food and gas.

CHAPTER

10

Threats to Righting the Path of Policy

Goals help you overcome short-term problems.[1]

—Hannah More

One can easily outline the changes that need to occur to put spending and taxes on a sustainable trajectory and reverse the excesses of American monetary policy. In practice, however, the path toward a more stable economic future is not straightforward. Not only does human nature tend toward short-term gratification, but the United States election cycle discourages politicians from making decisions for longer-term benefit, as well. Incentives for personal political gain are much higher than those for the public good. Even when the right choices are made, the results are not always as expected. Behavior is dynamic and changes as the environment evolves. Policies enacted with a particular goal in mind can result in very different consequences as human behavior, and markets, adapt.

Mobility Threatens Austerity

It's not surprising that most governors of American states are reluctant to raise taxes. Census data shows that states imposing relatively high income taxes, like New Jersey and New York, have experienced some of the lowest population gains in the country over the past decade, while low-tax states like Nevada, Texas, and Florida have grown the most. The chart in Figure 10.1 shows the

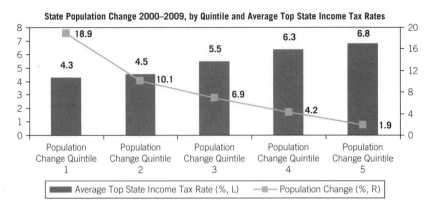

Figure 10.1　State Population Changes and Average Top State Tax Rates
Source: Census Bureau, Federation of Tax Administrators

simple relationship between tax rates and population changes between 2000 and 2009. There may be many other factors at play here, including favorable climate and cost of land, but on the surface there is a relationship between taxes and population migration.

The states ranking in the top 20 percent of population growth (Quintile 1) grew by 18.9 percent in the period and have, on average, the lowest top income tax bracket (4.3 percent) in the country. This group of states includes three—Florida, Nevada, and Texas—which have no state income tax at all. In fact, of the nine states with no income tax, all fell in the top half of rankings of state population growth. The average tax rate of the lowest-20 percent population-growth states, which grew by 1.9 percent, is 58 percent higher than that of the fastest-growing quintile.

Population mobility implies that raising state income tax rates may not result in an increase in revenues. Highly paid professionals, such as investment managers and entrepreneurs, are not necessarily tied to a particular location and çan easily move home base. Technology has made living almost anywhere feasible for people in knowledge-based professions. If the housing market stabilizes, mobility could increase in line with home values as people are able to sell with smaller losses or even small profits. It may seem farfetched that people would uproot their families based on taxes, but these conversations are taking place.

François took part in a dinner in 2010 attended mostly by hedge fund managers in Connecticut. The post-dinner conversation

Wolfe Trahan Client Survey

Would you consider/are you considering moving to a state or country with lower taxes: Yes or No?

Yes or No	Percentage
Would Consider Moving For Tax Reasons	35.1
Would Not Consider Moving For Tax Reasons	64.9

Survey conducted March 25, 2011.
Total respondents to this question: 724

centered on which states would have a more business-friendly environment for these high-income professionals to live. The zero-state-income-tax locations were compared based on weather, accessibility, schools, and culture. States like New Hampshire were crossed off due to weather, but a place like Tennessee was regarded as a high-quality option. Unless all states increase their tax rates by equivalent amounts—a highly unlikely scenario—governors may be reluctant to jump on the tax-hike bandwagon for fear of emigration which would make the fiscal situation even worse.

Revenue is not the only potential victim of mobility; states' political power is at risk as well. The congressional redistricting that occurs with the census every 10 years means that states losing population also lose seats in the House of Representatives. The slim margin each political party enjoys from time to time could be structurally changed if a particular party embraced tax hikes while the other did not. The result could be a barbelled power distribution among the states, as the higher-revenue states gain increasing clout, while the lower-revenue states drop in influence. As the wealthy congregate in lower tax states, and thus retain a greater portion of their income, the imbalances between income classes could grow even further. The likelihood could fall tremendously that members of Congress who represent these high-income constituents would vote for higher taxes. Even today we see this trend: each of the 10 wealthiest members of Congress—seven of whom are Democrats—voted to extend the Bush-era tax cuts.[2]

As a small percentage of the population gains a greater share of wealth, and by default, power, the more marginalized the lower economic strata become. As shown in Figure 10.2, the share of income earned by the top 1 percent of households increased 120 percent between 1979 and 2006, while the share earned by the bottom 20 percent of households fell more than 30 percent.

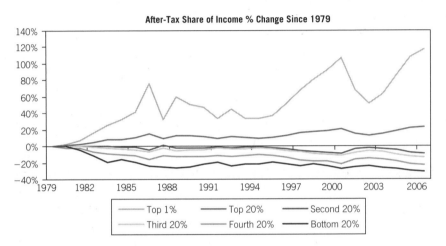

Figure 10.2   After-Tax Share of Income Has Increased for the Top 1 Percent of Earners
Source: Congressional Budget Office

Inequality and Protectionism

Several research studies have shown that it's not the absolute level of income that determines well being, but the perceived income level relative to others[3]. In other words, someone making $40,000 per year in a neighborhood where the average person makes $30,000 likely feels pretty good about his or her economic position. On the other hand, a person making $200,000 in a social or professional circle of seven-figure earners probably feels down and out. The income trends of the past several decades have already put the United States onto a path of greater inequality, and the policies of the last several years have exacerbated the situation. The weak-dollar policy of the Fed has encouraged higher commodity prices, which take a much larger bite out of lower-income families than wealthy ones. The impact of higher food prices on bottom-tier earners in the United States is equivalent to that felt in many emerging market countries.

Figure 10.3 illustrates the change in consumer confidence, as of February 2011, since Fed Chairman Bernanke announced QE2 in Jackson Hole in August 2010 and a new equity market rally began. Confidence soared for people in the high-income category as their stock holdings made them feel wealthier, meanwhile those in the low-income category grew less confident as food and energy prices took a larger chunk of their incomes.

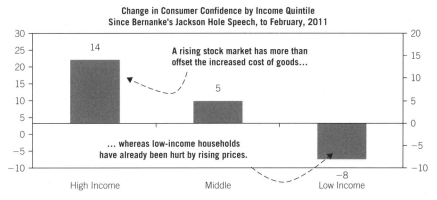

Change in Consumer Confidence by Income Quintile Since Bernanke's Jackson Hole Speech, to February, 2011

A rising stock market has more than offset the increased cost of goods...

... whereas low-income households have already been hurt by rising prices.

High Income   Middle   Low Income

Figure 10.3   Higher Food Prices Have a Huge Impact on Lower-Income Earners
Source: Wolfe Trahan & Co.

Monetary policy has encouraged a furious rally in the equity market, which has buoyed the wealth effect for those who are invested in stocks. Even fiscal policy has been lopsided. Measures such as the tax-cut extensions and the payroll tax holiday passed in late 2010 enable high earners to save more of their income while the lower income brackets must spend these tax savings to scrape by. The spending cuts and tax increases necessary to right the current policy mistakes could actually exacerbate the negative employment environment, causing even more distress for those who live paycheck to paycheck. Economic hardships tend to incline people and nations to turn inward and defensive instead of outward and cooperative. Much of the world's growth over the past several decades has been attributable to greater globalization and free-trade policies around the world. Marginalizing the have-nots threatens these positive trends and raises the specter of return to protectionism and stifled trade.

The effects are not limited to the United States. Rising food prices resulting from the Fed's ultra-easy monetary policy have ushered in a new era of protectionist sentiment around the world. Currency devaluations, both implicit and explicit, show the desire to remain competitive at the expense of other nations. China keeps its Yuan pegged to the dollar at a time when Chinese growth far outpaces America's, artificially depressing the cost of Chinese goods in the global marketplace. Vietnam explicitly devalued its currency in February 2011 to improve its trade shortfall as the economy took a blow from higher inflation. Fearing a repeat of the food riots in 2007 and 2008, Myanmar halted exports of rice to help keep the domestic price in check. Moves such as these are signs that governments are quick to protect their local economies to the potential detriment of the global market.

In Europe, the recession and the fiscal crises of Greece, Portugal, Ireland, and several other countries have elicited defensive, retributive political actions. Recent elections have seen many governments adopt more nationalistic platforms. Ireland kicked out the party that has dominated its politics since 1921, while the far-right Sinn Fein, the political wing of the Irish Republican Army, gained seats in Parliament on the back of an anti-Europe, anti-banker campaign. The Turkish Prime Minister made waves by urging Turks living in Germany to learn Turkish before learning German.

Business Cycle Trends Could Exacerbate the Policy Conundrum

The inflationary pressures making their way from Asia, through Europe, and eventually to the United States threaten to slow global economic recovery. If growth and employment begin to erode again in the United States, the likelihood of tighter fiscal policy is nil. Faced with slowing growth but rising inflation, the future actions of the Federal Reserve are unpredictable. Additional easing would only exacerbate the inflation problem, but tightening would further choke off consumer spending and employment growth.

The scenario for America is quite different today than it would have been a decade ago. Now that commodity prices and the business cycle are no longer in synch, the inflation/deflation tradeoff is far more complicated. In the past, rising commodity prices would have accompanied red-hot growth and acted as reinforcement to tighter monetary policy. Today, higher prices are an unintended consequence. Going forward, the most likely scenario is one in which the United States experiences a bout of inflationary pressure, and, due to the already low-growth environment, this will likely lead to deflationary policies.

Chapter Summary

- The path toward a more stable economic future is not straightforward. The United States election cycle discourages politicians from making decisions for longer-term benefit, as well, and incentives for personal political gain are much higher than those for the public good.
- Mobility threatens austerity: Census data shows that the lowest income tax states had the highest population growth over the past decade.
- The income trends of the past several decades have already put the United States onto a path of greater inequality, and the policies of the last several years have exacerbated the situation.
- Since Fed Chairman Bernanke announced QE2 in August 2010 and a new equity market rally began, confidence soared for people in the high-income category. Those in the low-income category grew less confident as food and energy prices took a larger chunk of their income.

PART

IV

INVESTING FOR AN UNCERTAIN FUTURE

Most investors would agree that the years since the onset of the Great Recession have been challenging. During that period, some of the financial industry's biggest firms collapsed, millions of people lost their homes and jobs, fortunes were destroyed (and made), and the United States government essentially commandeered the financial system. Macro forces, such as the rise and fall of the dollar and employment trends, dominated market movements even as many large, non-bank corporations weathered the recession with healthy balance sheets. During and since this time, investing successfully has boiled down to getting the big picture right first and foremost, and then building an underlying portfolio which benefits from the macro environment.

As the global economy continues to evolve past the credit crisis, investors are adapting to newfound "truths": Housing prices don't always go up; the United States no longer controls commodity markets; and enough government spending can carry equities higher, at least for some period of time. They are also re-learning the lesson that there is no free lunch. Anything bought on credit must be paid for eventually, whether that is a house, a pair of jeans, or an economic recovery. This is obvious to most Americans, although apparently it is not obvious to politicians. If the bill comes due and payback is not possible, then the purchase will likely be taken away. Much of the world is now staring the bill for the economic recovery in the face, and looking for someone to cover the tab.

Savvy investors should never have doubted that the bill for the recession and its recovery would come due. Just like any other bubble in history, the excesses had to be undone before renewal could take place. *Unlike* most other bubbles, however, the excesses were so systemic that their unwinding nearly brought down the financial system as a whole. The amount of government stimulus provided to keep the system functioning was enormous, and has added an extra layer of complexity to navigating the markets. Now, investors have to grapple with the unpredictable decisions and timing of policy makers, and how their actions affect global markets. The uncertainty remains today, and in all likelihood, will shadow the markets for some time.

Under these circumstances, it is difficult to forecast a precise path for financial markets during the years to come. The myriad of decisions yet to be made by central bankers around the world, not to mention unpredictable geopolitical developments, will greatly influence the financial future. There is, however, a macro framework that investors can use to prepare their portfolios for the inflationary and deflationary scenarios most likely to evolve over the next several years. Certainly a path is already set in motion, one that looks decidedly inflationary in the near term, but circumstances can change quickly. The reactionary nature of policy tends to lead markets from one extreme to the next. *The global inflationary pressures resulting from the Fed's weak-dollar policy will likely result in a growth slowdown and a future disinflationary, if not deflationary, period.* The timing is uncertain, but understanding how to read macro trends, and shift a portfolio accordingly, will enable investors to navigate choppy waters and benefit from both inflationary and deflationary cycles as they unfold.

11

A Closer Look at Inflation

Inflation is taxation without legislation.[1]

—Milton Friedman

The mechanism that transforms money supply growth into inflation can take several forms, but usually boils down to two things: the money multiplier and the currency. The inflation issue facing the United States has to do with the latter.

The Fed's primary responsibility is monetary policy, so it is intuitive that the trickle-down effect of loose policy begins with money supply. Since quantitative easing began in 2009, money supply has grown in lockstep with the Fed's balance sheet. Bank lending, however, has not grown similarly. Lending has recovered somewhat from the recessionary deep-freeze, but neither *supply of* nor *demand for* credit has fully returned. Banks have chosen to repair their balance sheets by building up balances rather than lending funds, and consumers have chosen to deleverage instead of borrow. More than two years past the onset of the recession, revolving credit was still at cycle lows.

Inflationary pressures emerged as a result of ultra-stimulative policy, but not because of an excessive demand for money. Instead, inflationary pressures resulted from the weak dollar. As money supply was increased in an attempt to stimulate demand, investors grew concerned about a debasement of the currency. Downward pressure on the currency was exacerbated as the Fed continued to signal that it would keep easy policy in place as long as possible, while other central banks began moving toward tighter policy. Capital flowed toward countries where expectations for higher interest rates increased and away from the near-zero-yielding dollar. Costs of commodities priced in dollars were driven up by the weaker currency, which fueled inflation in heavy commodity-consuming countries like China. By early 2011, higher input prices were gradually being exported from the East toward the West.

Anatomy of Inflation in the United States

The main driver of the divergence in policy between the United States and the rest of the world in the aftermath of the credit crisis is the Fed's unique focus on core inflation. While food and energy prices skyrocketed around the world, American core inflation—which excludes both food and energy—remained relatively subdued. The stability of the underlying inflation measure allowed the Fed to brush off hawkish critics and justify its continuation of quantitative easing. Once Fed officials finally admitted that there was a serious recession taking place in 2008, fear of deflation became their steady mantra.

Fear of deflation was valid and justified for a time, but for policy makers to say that inflation is a good outcome is beyond comprehension. Indeed though, the Fed's actions have borne out this preference. The United States is now faced with the worst kind of inflation—import price inflation. This type of inflation is not in any way similar to wage gains, which have some benefits to the nation. Rising import prices act purely as a regressive tax on lower-income consumers, or only those people who have to eat and drive a car to make it in the world. The more the Fed has eased, the lower the dollar has fallen, and the higher the prices of food and energy products have risen. Certainly, the increasing amount of protein in the diet of the Chinese or acres planted of certain foods influence longer-term changes, but macro trends like these do not cause dramatic price increases overnight.

The role the Fed has played in the commodity rally is larger than many people realize. The Fed's easy policy has become binding; the United States economy is addicted to stimulus, and the bank's myopic focus on core inflation has allowed this to occur. In the minds of policy makers, they are goosing the engine and gaining little speed, causing them to push even harder on the accelerator. Meanwhile, the rest of the car is ready to overheat.

The factors that drive inflation can differ fairly significantly from country to country depending on the make-up of the inflation index. In the United States, as shown in Figure 11.1, the overall total Consumer Price Index (CPI) is dominated by two groups of prices: Food and energy, which make up almost 23 percent of the index, and rent, which accounts for nearly 30 percent.

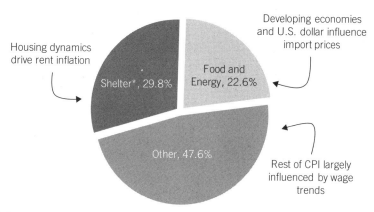

*Shelter = Owners Equivalent Rent + Rent of primary residence.

Figure 11.1   Understanding Inflation Statistics in the United States
Source: Wolfe Trahan & Co.

The remaining portion of the headline measure is largely influenced by trends in wages, so even outside of the pricing pressures of food and energy, the economy is vulnerable to rising housing costs and wages. A good leading indicator for inflation historically has been the performance of apartment Real Estate Investment Trusts (REITs). The strong performance of apartment REITs as of the first quarter of 2011 implies an uptick in the shelter component of inflation, while gains in unit labor costs suggest a rise in core inflation excluding shelter. These trends herald an increase in the *core* inflation index, and are evidence that the Fed should be turning its attention toward price stability instead of consumer spending.

Despite the malaise lingering in the housing market after the end of the recession, lower apartment vacancy rates and better pricing power is returning to this area of the housing market, as seen in Figure 11.2. The chart shows the close relationship between the change in the apartment vacancy rate and the movement in

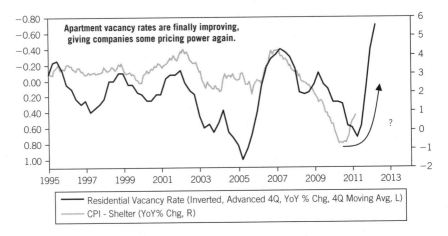

Figure 11.2   The Market for Apartments Firming Up
Source: Wolfe Trahan & Co.

the shelter component of inflation a year later. The same pattern appears when looking at the performance of apartment REITs. A surge in apartment REIT performance historically has indicated that a corresponding rise in rent inflation is not far behind. With shelter comprising nearly 40 percent of core inflation, this could be an impactful trend.

The remainder of core inflation, outside of shelter, boils down to wage trends. Changes in unit labor costs tend to move in the same direction as inflation excluding shelter, as shown in Figure 11.3. Headlines bemoaning the dismal labor market have led many to believe that wage pressures are nonexistent, but this is no longer the case. The unemployment rate remains high, but the trend is improving. As the labor market tightened, unit labor costs have started to rise. More than 650,000 workers in Colorado, Washington, Montana, Arizona, Ohio, Oregon, and Vermont received pay raises in 2011 due to increased minimum wages. If these trends continue, core CPI should follow suit.

Fed Chairman Bernanke has claimed that the central bank has the tools to fight inflation at a moment's notice if pressures appear in the core index. While the Fed does have the tools, it's the timing that is questionable. Core inflation is a lagging indicator. The effects of past stimulus remain in play long after policy measures

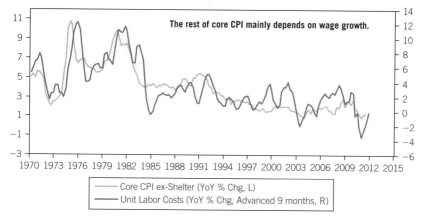

Figure 11.3   Outside of Rent, Core Inflation Boils Down to Wages
Source: Wolfe Trahan & Co.

Figure 11.4   The Lagged Effects of Stimulus Could Lift Core Inflation
Source: Wolfe Trahan & Co.

are enacted, and impact official inflation statistics with a significant time lag, as shown in Figure 11.4.

The *Firms Raising Prices* component from the NFIB Survey of Small Business highlights how pricing pressures filter through to inflation. Once firms begin to experience some pricing power, it takes more than a year for these higher prices to show up in the inflation data, as shown in Figure 11.5. The time gap holds when reigning in policy as well—tightening policy today does not

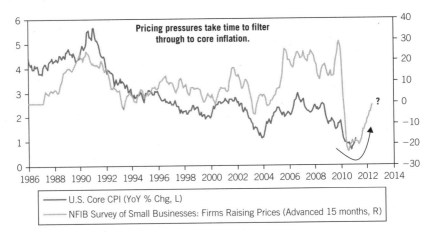

Figure 11.5   Pricing Power Feeds Through to "Official" Inflation with a Lag
Source: Wolfe Trahan & Co.

dampen inflation for several quarters. If the Fed wanted to preempt core inflation from becoming a problem a year down the road, the time to withdraw liquidity was yesterday.

The Consumer IS Exposed to Food and Energy

Despite the Fed's reliance on core inflation as a policy guide, the American consumer is highly exposed to food and energy prices. While these two groups make up just less than 23 percent of the total consumer price index, their price movements explain 80 percent of the variation in the index! Figure 11.6 illustrates that food and energy are by far the most volatile components of inflation; they have oscillated in a 30-percentage-point range since 2000. By comparison, housing inflation has varied by only six percentage points over the same time period, and all other prices had a range of four percentage points.

Food and energy prices have a major impact on overall inflation, and they go hand in hand with import price inflation, as shown in Figure 11.7. The U.S. economy derives more than 70 percent of its GDP from personal consumption, and it imports a huge portion of the goods consumed. As the inputs to these goods become more expensive, domestic inflation tends to increase. This relationship has been very tight for several decades, and increasing globalization should only increase the correlation. Those people

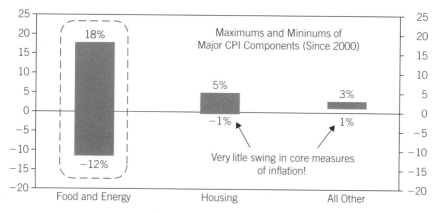

Figure 11.6   Food and Energy Are the Most Volatile Components of Inflation
Source: Wolfe Trahan & Co.

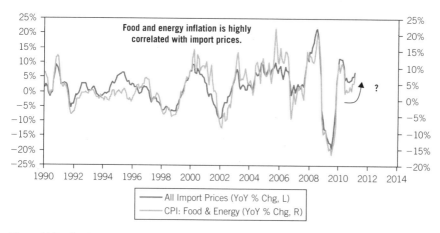

Figure 11.7   Food and Energy Are Closely Related to Import Prices
Source: Wolfe Trahan & Co.

who argue that food and energy do not impact headline inflation are not considering the indirect effects through imports of many different types of products.

Anecdotal evidence of inflation pressures in core goods is mounting. Companies have been absorbing much of the input price increases for several quarters, but by late 2010 many began suggesting that they would raise consumer prices to help offset the pain their margins have been experiencing. Figure 11.8 gives some company-specific examples of how higher commodity prices are forcing the hands of corporations in many diverse industries.

Electrical Equipment

Regal Beloit Corporation [RBC] on Q4 earnings: "We implemented price increases to offset the inflation" but couldn't raise prices fast enough to head off a decline in profits.

Specialty Retail

Abercrombie And Fitch [ANF] Feb 2011: "I think that's the question of the day. We know that we have to counter cost increases, the question is how much."

Containers and Packaging

Greif (GEF) 3/2/11: "Cost pass-through mechanisms in our sales contracts helped to mitigate the impact of inflation in raw materials."

Airlines

United Continental (UAL) 2/23/11: United Continental's United Airlines unveiled a $20 round-trip fuel surcharge on most domestic routes matched by AMR Corp.'s American Airlines.

Air Freight and Logistics

FedEx Fuel Surcharge: The fuel surcharge percentage for FedEx Ground services is subject to monthly adjustment based on a rounded average of the national U.S. on-highway average price for a gallon of diesel fuel.

Textiles, Apparel, and Luxury Goods

Clothing manufacturer for Polo Ralph Lauren and Le Coq Sportif 11/16/2010: "If cotton keeps rising like this, we will need to lift prices by 30 percent by the Spring Festival next year or we lose money."

Figure 11.8   Rising Commodity Prices Will Ultimately Impact Core Goods
Source: Wolfe Trahan & Co.

Policies to Avoid Deflation Often Lead to Inflation

A critical issue for the path of policy during and immediately after the Great Recession was the debate between inflation and deflation. The deflation camp, rallied by Fed Chairman Bernanke, adamantly and vehemently defended pouring stimulus into the markets by citing the dangers of downward-spiraling prices similar to Japan in the 1990s. Despite a sharp rally in the stock market, weak employment and a stagnant housing market kept core inflation too low for the Fed's comfort.

On the other side, the inflation camp worried that massive expansion of the money supply resulting from a zero interest rate policy, quantitative easing, and a weak dollar would eventually spark pricing pressures and stall the nascent recovery. They argued that despite the weak labor market and lack of immediate-term pricing pressures in the United States, the Fed's policies would have inflationary consequences around the world.

In reality, the debate has been less about *what* to do than about *when to stop* doing it. Very few people denied that a drastic policy response was required to keep the economy from falling deeper into recession in 2008. The Federal Reserve's infamous aversion to deflation left little doubt that the central bank would act aggressively and swiftly, and they did. GDP growth rebounded sharply in the second half of 2009, but by the spring of 2010 the recovery plateaued. The burst from stimulus was past its peak and fiscal problems in Europe were starting to weigh on investor confidence worldwide. At this point, the inflation and deflation camps seriously diverged. The deflationists called for more stimulus to reignite the recovery and boost employment, which continued to lag, and the inflationists believed that more easy policy would lead to inflation down the road. Inflation pressures were already simmering in early 2010, however; the commodity complex had begun its upward trajectory in early 2009, as shown in Figure 11.9. Not coincidentally, the Fed had launched its first round of quantitative easing in November 2008.

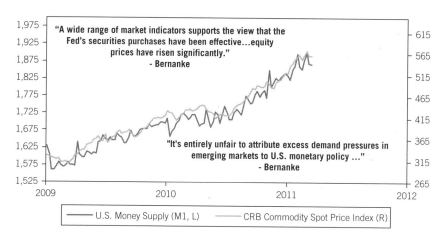

Figure 11.9   Commodity Prices Have Risen in Lockstep with Money Supply Growth
Source: Wolfe Trahan & Co.

Not until protests rocked oil-producing nations in North Africa and the Middle East in early 2011 did many investors even view inflation as a concern. Many people blamed the unrest for causing oil prices to run. Those events were only the catalyst that drew attention to rising commodity prices, not the cause. The argument that the uprisings were responsible for the oil rally would be more convincing if oil alone had spiked. Similarly, those who point to the emerging middle class in China as the sole force behind rising food prices would have more credibility if only corn was skyrocketing. The reality was that commodities as diverse as sugar, soybeans, cotton, platinum, and tin were soaring, as seen in Figure 11.10, all propelled by the weak dollar.

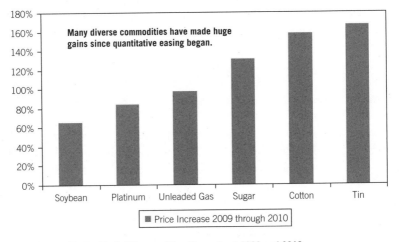

Figure 11.10   The Dollar Fueled Commodities Throughout 2009 and 2010
Source: DJUBS

It is sometimes unclear what Chairman Bernanke is trying to say in these matters, but it often sounds as if he is denying that the Fed had a role in the commodity price rally at all. The crux of the disagreement is his claim that the commodity rally is the result of increased demand from emerging countries, instead of the artificially suppressed dollar. At the National Press Club in Washington in February 2011 he was quoted as saying,

> It's entirely unfair to attribute excess demand pressures in emerging markets to U.S. monetary policy, because emerging markets have all the tools they need to address excess demand in those countries.

> *Chairman Ben S. Bernanke at the National Press Club,*
> *Washington, D.C., February 3, 2011*

He elaborated on his rather defensive remark in Congressional testimony a few days later,

> Indeed, prices of many industrial and agricultural commodities have risen lately, largely as a result of the very strong demand from fast-growing emerging market economies, coupled, in some cases, with constraints on supply.
>
> *Chairman Ben S. Bernanke before the Committee on the Budget, U.S. House of Representatives, Washington, D.C., February 9, 2011*

Regardless of the cause, there is no debate that food prices are at a record high, shown in Figure 11.11. Prices at these levels have a significant negative impact on consumers in emerging economies, and their central banks have started acting to reverse the trend. As of the end of the first quarter, central banks in 20 countries had already hiked rates in 2011, with two of the world's biggest exporters (China and South Korea) tightening policy multiple times.

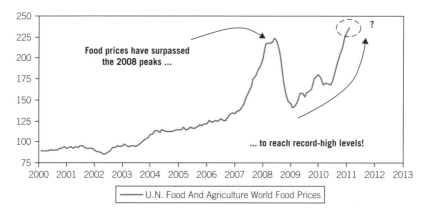

Figure 11.11   Record-High Food Prices are Putting Pressure on Foreign Central Banks to Tighten

Pricing pressures in Asia easily filter out to the rest of the world through trade. Higher commodities translate into higher input prices for manufacturers, which are embedded in the goods exporters like China sell to other countries. In order to keep the country's exports competitive, China is notoriously vigilant in combating inflation. Pricing pressures in the economy mean that the People's Bank of China raises interest rates, with little exception. Figure 11.12 shows

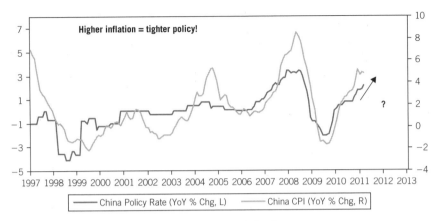

Figure 11.12   Higher Inflation in China Begets Higher Policy Rates
Source: Wolfe Trahan & Co.

the tight correlation between the country's inflation rate and policy rates.

The conundrum for the American central bank is how to react when it would prefer global interest rates to be falling instead of rising. As the world economy becomes even more globalized, policy decisions in other countries have a strong influence on economic prospects in the United States. As shown in Figure 11.13, the more short-term interest rates rise abroad, the further leading indicators in the United States are likely to decline. Inflationary pressures spreading from Asia into Europe could be the spark needed to fuel even more rate hikes across the globe. If higher prices filter onto American shores before the domestic economy fully recovers, the Fed will face a no-win situation. Maintaining accommodative policy as the rest of the world raises interest rates keeps the dollar low and further fans the flames of domestic inflation. Alternatively, tightening policy chokes off the domestic recovery. Either way, the American consumer faces significant headwinds.

An alternative scenario is possible in which significant inflation does not materialize in the United States. Tightening measures well underway in the East could cool growth so much that those exports dry up quickly, although this is unlikely since pricing pressures have been in the pipeline for some time. If that were to happen though, the problem then becomes one of weak global demand. The United States recovery is still precarious, and a slowdown

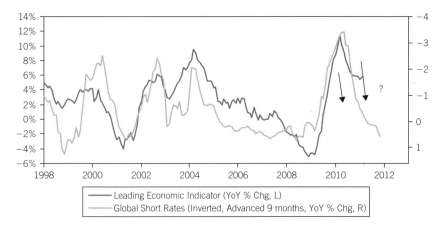

Figure 11.13   Global Policy Lays the Tracks for Leading Economic Indicators in the United States
Source: Wolfe Trahan & Co.

in the rest of the world could stamp out any contribution that American exports could provide to GDP. This would likely result in a "double dip" scenario. At that point, the push for new stimulus could begin again, but from a much more dangerous fiscal starting point.

Neither of these outcomes is desirable. While many factors could mitigate these circumstances, the most likely scenario is one in which the United States experiences bouts of both inflation and deflation in coming years. Inflation does not need to reach 1970s-era double-digits to become a problem. An upward trend of a few percentage points could cause investors to extrapolate higher prices and cause inflation expectations to rise significantly. There is little doubt that an increase in inflation expectations would prompt the Federal Reserve to raise interest rates, and if history is a guide, they likely will overshoot. If food and energy inflation continues to outpace wage gains, the likely result will be a growth slowdown followed by disinflation at best, and deflation at worst.

Pushing on a String

Many emerging countries learned valuable lessons during the currency crisis that swept Asia in the late 1990s and, as a result, improved the resiliency of their balance sheets and financial systems in the following years. These economies were still dealt a blow from the global recession in 2008, but bounced back much more quickly without having to shoulder the heavy burden of deleveraging. This difference in resiliency put the United States and Asia on different tracks after the recession, with China recovering strongly and quickly. Although the Federal Reserve intended to pull the American economy from the quicksand of the Great Recession, the Fed instead fueled the simmering fire of the Asian economic recovery, an unintended consequence of sustained, ultra-easy policies.

In essence, the global economic balance had shifted, but Fed policy had not. The Fed continued to pursue policies that weighed on the value of the dollar and helped drive commodity prices through the roof. Since the United States is no longer the price setter for commodities, the slow recovery was not in synch with the rising prices. This had not been the case in previous recoveries. Instead of helping pull the United States out of recession, commodities acted in opposition to the stimulus that fed their gains, resulting in the equivalent of the Fed pushing on a string.

As of the first quarter of 2011, strong corporate earnings have helped overshadow macro headwinds. Macro pressures should take the upper hand in time as inflationary pressures crimp the supply chain from start to finish. The turning point for leading indicators already has arrived in China after many months of inflation and tightening pressures, as shown in Figure 11.14. The question is how quickly these pressures will travel from East to West.

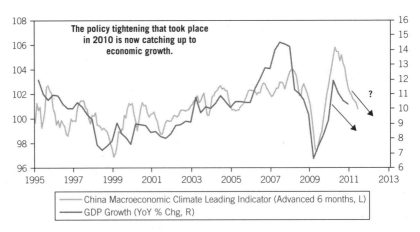

Figure 11.14   China's Leading Indicators Are Sliding Lower
Source: Wolfe Trahan & Co.

The Fed will be chasing its tail on policy until a weak dollar stops contributing to inflationary pressures. From a forty-thousand-foot view, there are two scenarios that are likely to be dollar-bullish:

1. An end to policy tightening in the emerging world, or
2. A definitive end to quantitative easing in the United States, or even better, a non-zero policy rate.

Emerging economies are unlikely to stop raising rates as long as inflation is a threat. Absent a major shock, the Fed will have difficulty maintaining its easing bias. The second round of quantitative easing is set to expire in June 2011, and at this point an extension looks unlikely. One of the ways Chairman Bernanke has distinguished himself from former Chairman Alan Greenspan is his willingness to provide a clear message; the public knows where he stands on the outlook for policy. It's also clear from the outspokenness of the regional Fed governors that there are multiple views within the policy-setting committee, and there definitely is a voice for withdrawing stimulus. Figure 11.15 shows some of the dissension within the ranks of the Fed.

Figure 11.15   Dissension Growing Among the Fed Governors
Source: Wolfe Trahan & Co.

It will be a key turning point when the Fed withdraws its policy tailwind. The S&P 500 has grown dependent on a lower dollar, and it will be difficult for equities to trend higher if the dollar reverses course. A negative market reaction would likely coincide with leading indicators rolling over as well. At that point Treasuries would provide better returns than equities.

Inflation has Social and Political Consequences

The percentage of world GDP generated in countries tied to the dollar is as high as it has ever been. Figure 11.16 shows that it weighs in at 12.4 percent, and represents the largest share of world GDP other than the United States. Most importantly, the current price setter of commodities—China—is a member of the group tied to the dollar. Quite simply, a lower dollar fuels inflation in China by artificially depressing its currency, the Yuan. This is equivalent to giving a dose of steroids to an economy that is already humming. The extra kick has boosted Chinese growth and fed the demand for commodities. *Inflation in a country that is the beginning of the world's supply chain starts a domino effect likely to eventually reach American shores.*

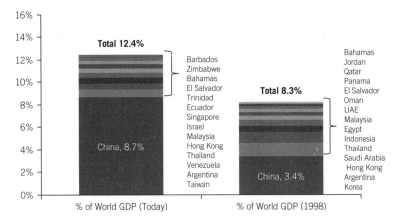

Figure 11.16   Percentage of Global GDP Pegged to the Dollar Is on the Rise
Source: Wolfe Trahan & Co.

Chairman Bernanke has minimized the link between bank policy and inflation overseas, but in actuality he is not arguing that the weak dollar has no effect on the Chinese economy. Rather, he believes that the People's Bank of China possesses the tools necessary to combat over-heating growth. In *theory*, the Chinese could remove the Yuan's peg to the dollar and allow their currency to float freely in the market. In *reality*, this would cause an abrupt revaluation of the Yuan and result in dramatically tighter conditions in China, effectively slamming the brakes on the world's growth engine. The result would be drastically higher unemployment and unrest in China. The likelihood that China would act on a measure with such severe consequences is nil. Any Chinese official watching the news out of Northern Africa is well aware of the disastrous consequences of structurally high unemployment.

Meanwhile, in the United States the main beneficiary of the weaker dollar has not been consumer spending or income growth, but the equity market. While the equity rally has enhanced the wealth of Americans who own stocks, a large segment of the population that most needed an economic boost has been excluded. Making matters worse, lower-income Americans spend a higher percentage of their income on food than those at the upper end, making them more vulnerable to rising commodity prices. In fact, the food spending patterns in America's lower income brackets are more in line with those of emerging market countries than the average in the United States. Figure 11.17 details the spending by income bracket. Households earning more than $70,000 per year spend about 9 percent of their budgets on food, but those earning less than $20,000 per year spend more than 30 percent on food. This high level is similar to that of Mexico, Brazil, and emerging countries in Eastern Europe.

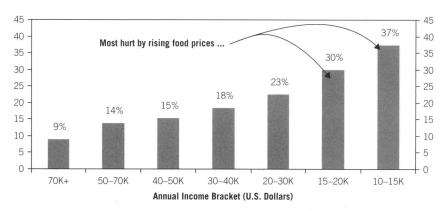

Figure 11.17   Share of Annual Household Income Spent on Food Varies Significantly by Income
Source: Wolfe Trahan & Co.

It is no coincidence that the equity markets in countries which spend the greatest amount on food have underperformed wealthier nations through the first quarter of 2011. Figure 11.18 shows the divergence. The World Bank recently said that "rising food prices

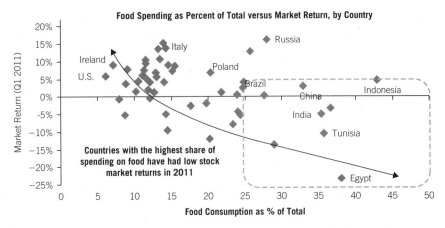

Figure 11.18   Markets Most Exposed to Food Prices Had the Weakest Stock Markets in First Quarter 2011

Source: Wolfe Trahan & Co.

have driven an estimated 44 million people into poverty in developing countries" since June 2010.[2] Without a doubt, Americans in the lower income brackets have also underperformed their higher-income counterparts.

Higher gasoline prices also put the squeeze on disposable income. Some back-of-the-envelope calculations show that the dollar's depreciation trimmed about 1.5 percent from consumers' disposable incomes from 2008 to 2011. That is a significant, regressive tax which makes the price of creating export-related jobs very expensive overall. The chart in Figure 11.19 shows that consumers are already tilting their consumption toward necessary items, leaving less room for discretionary purchases. The strain on consumers is also eroding savings.

Fiscal and trade policy at the national level is also affected by inflation. An inflation-weakened consumer makes it more difficult for politicians to pursue austerity in the form of spending cuts and tax hikes. It would be highly unpopular to cut unemployment benefits or food stamp programs when many Americans are struggling to feed their families, regardless of the political party in control. Although Chairman Bernanke calls for Congress to get the fiscal house in order, his policies make that more difficult than necessary. Protectionism can take hold as countries impose export restrictions

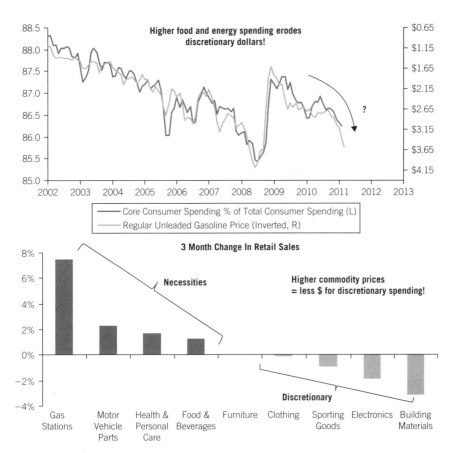

Figure 11.19   Higher Oil Prices Coincide with Fewer Discretionary Dollars
Source: Wolfe Trahan & Co., Bloomberg

and tariffs to keep domestic prices down, further raising prices for goods in the global market. While the risk of deflation is one that should absolutely be avoided, the downside of inflation is significant as well.

Market Indications of Inflation

The equity market is an excellent gauge of when the bite of inflation is really being felt, particularly with regard to the dollar. There is a tipping point for a weaker dollar; it helps until it hurts. The tailwind for equities reverses when the weaker currency boosts import prices enough to become a tax on consumers' spending behavior. Looking back to the 2006 through 2008 period, equities began to decline around the point when oil reached $95 per barrel and gasoline reached $3.10 per gallon. The 2010 and 2011 oil price run is repeating that pattern. When the weight of oil is too much for equities to bear, inflation is taking its toll.

Within the equity market, a change in sector leadership can indicate when inflation is prompting a move away from business cycle expansion. The relative performance of early-to-late stage cyclical sectors is the relationship to watch. Early-stage cyclicals are heavily consumer oriented, and therefore bear the brunt of inflationary pressures first. They typically begin to underperform six months prior to a decline in leading economic indicators (LEIs). This relationship accurately predicted the recovery in LEIs, and the equity market, that occurred in late 2010. The relative performance of early-to-late cyclicals began deteriorating in the United States in the first half of 2011, signaling a coming peak in LEIs.

Inflation indicators do not necessarily need to be domestically oriented; foreign markets also provide information. An uptick in Chinese inflation foretells higher interest rates, and a corresponding decline in leading indicators. This process has already begun as of early 2011.

The inflation and growth disconnect in Europe stands as an example of the dilemma the United States may face. The region's money supply growth has taken a nose dive, as shown in Figure 11.20, signaling lower GDP growth ahead. The European Central Bank

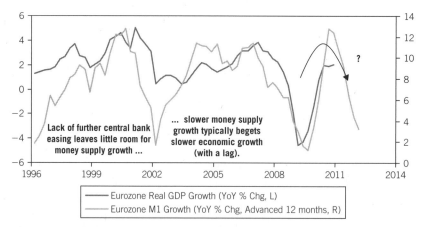

Figure 11.20   Declining Money Supply Growth Implies Slower GDP Growth Ahead in Europe
Source: Wolfe Trahan & Co.

(ECB) should normally be easing policy to avoid a severe decline in economic growth, but inflationary pressures are a fly in the ointment. Food and energy make up almost 30 percent of the Eurozone's pricing gauge, and inflation in Europe has accelerated since mid-2009, as shown in Figure 11.21. The ECB maintains a strict anti-inflation mandate, but focusing on rising prices could inhibit the appropriate monetary response for an impending decline in growth.

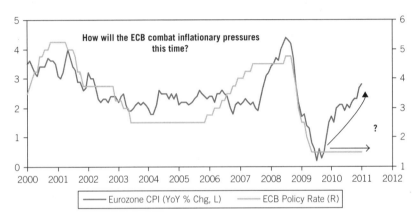

Figure 11.21   Inflation in Europe Began Rising in Mid-2009
Source: Wolfe Trahan & Co.

Information directly from businesses also provides a critical gauge of inflationary pressures. Evidence from the regional manufacturing surveys, like the Philly Fed Index, shows when inflation pressures are rising to problematic levels. Taking the difference between the *Prices Received* component of the Philly Fed index and the *Prices Paid* component results in a line that closely resembles actual inflation in the United States. As shown in Figure 11.22, this inflation proxy appears to be heading north. An increase in Prices Paid without a corresponding increase in Prices Received tends to weigh on another subcomponent of the index, *New Orders*. The New Orders component has the longest lead time of all the underlying series, roughly a six-month window, and therefore is an important early sign of growth trends. As of early 2011, the Prices Paid components of many regional surveys had risen to 30-year highs. This development does not bode well for general business conditions down the road, and is a sign that a peak in leading indicators could be imminent.

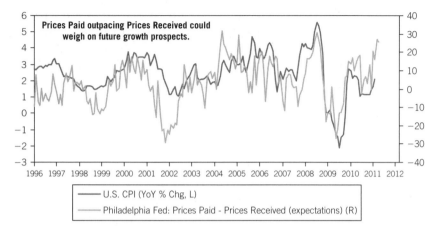

Figure 11.22   **Prices Paid Rising Faster Than Prices Received Could Signal Slower Growth Ahead**
Source: Wolfe Trahan & Co.

Chapter Summary

- The unpredictable decisions and timing of policy makers will shadow the financial markets for some time. Under these circumstances, it is difficult to forecast a precise path for markets, but investors can use macro to prepare for the inflationary and deflationary scenarios most likely to evolve in the years to come.
- Investing successfully has boiled down to getting the big picture right first and foremost, and then building an underlying portfolio which benefits from the macro environment.
- The Fed's prolonged easy policy has weakened the dollar and driven up commodity prices. Policy makers' myopic focus on core inflation, which excludes food and energy prices, has allowed this to occur.
- Fed officials express disbelief that their policies are responsible for food and energy inflation, and instead look toward demand from emerging markets. The increasing amount of protein in the diet of the Chinese or acres planted of certain foods influence longer-term changes, but macro trends like these do not cause dramatic price increases overnight.

- The effects of past stimulus remain in play long after policy measures are enacted, and impact official inflation statistics with a significant time lag.
- If food and energy inflation continues to outpace wage gains, the likely result will be a growth slowdown followed by disinflation at best, and deflation at worst.

CHAPTER

12

Strategies for Investing in Inflationary and Deflationary Environments

A free-enterprise economy depends only on markets, and according to the most advanced mathematical macroeconomic theory, markets depend only on moods: specifically, the mood of the men in the pinstripes, also known as the Boys on the Street. When the Boys are in a good mood, the market thrives; when they get scared or sullen, it is time for each one of us to look into the retail apple business.[1]

—Barbara Ehrenreich

The asset allocation consequences of higher inflation are not as clear cut as many believe. Some investors would argue stocks are a big beneficiary of inflation and it often means greater pricing power for all companies, but this is not necessarily the case. Inflation is a headwind, not a tailwind, to equity market multiples and company margins. Put simply, inflation is a growth depressant. A rise in inflation is often followed by a drop in leading indicators of the economy.

Investing appropriately for a higher-inflation environment should be a two-stage event. The first period occurs while inflation expectations are rising and pricing pressures are building in the economy. During this stage investors should be most concerned about protecting their portfolios from the impact of inflation. Many investors are aware of the assets that perform well in the first stage,

Wolfe Trahan Client Survey

What are you more worried about in the next several years: Inflation or Deflation?

Primary Concern	Percentage
Inflation	88.7
Deflation	11.3

Survey conducted March 25, 2011.
Total respondents to this question: 725

and therefore it is called the stage of *Conventional Wisdom*. Once inflation emerges and consumers feel the impact of higher prices, the second stage has arrived. Although investors should then prepare their portfolios for a slowdown, many miss this shift, are misallocated, and thus fail to benefit from slowing growth. This stage is called *Making the Turn*.

Conventional Wisdom—Hedging for Higher Inflation

There is a conventional wisdom among investors regarding how to invest in the face of rising inflation. Most believe that bonds should be avoided as yields rise to compensate for higher inflation, driving down their prices. Companies with the ability to raise prices and pass the inflation on to consumers become popular stock choices. Inflation is also one of the macro forces that matters most when it comes to sector rotation. Equity sector leadership rotates from consumer-driven, early cyclical sectors into late cyclicals like energy, industrials, and materials as prices start to rise. This is usually the proper positioning, but getting the timing correct is a challenge. Most investors are late to move into these areas and then late to exit when the backdrop shifts again.

The underperformance of early cyclical sectors, most often visible in consumer discretionary stocks, is a key indicator that inflationary pressures are increasing. The chart in Figure 12.1 highlights the relationship between the rate of inflation and the relative performance of late cyclicals to early cyclicals. The correlation is tight: An upturn in inflation is nearly coincident with late cyclical sectors outperforming early cyclical sectors. The logic behind the sector rotation is intuitive. As the prices of goods and services go up, stocks reliant on the consumer come under pressure. A larger share of disposable income is diverted toward necessities, which takes a bite out of discretionary consumer spending. This is particularly true when essentials like food and energy are experiencing inflated prices. Basically, inflation acts as a tax on consumers and discretionary purchases are the first to be cut. Alternatively, stocks that are less vulnerable to changes in consumption patterns, like energy, perform better.

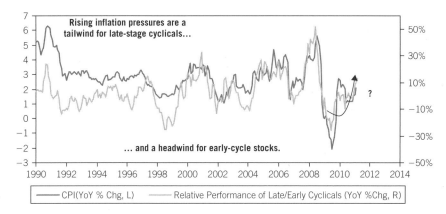

Figure 12.1   Rising Inflation Pressures Provide a Tailwind for Late-Stage Cyclicals
Source: Wolfe Trahan & Co.

It is important to remember that the United States is three standard deviations above the global average in share of the economy derived from consumption, and it has the third-lowest share of growth attributable to exports. When pricing pressures emerge, it is best to avoid domestically oriented, consumer-driven areas in the near term, and prepare for a general slowdown in the medium term. Late-stage cyclical companies tend to have more exposure abroad, and thus benefit from a declining dollar and rising infla-tion. Energy, industrials, and materials are all sectors that tend to benefit from rising inflation. Figure 12.2 shows the sector break-down of early and late stage cyclical groups.

Wall Street analysts usually lag in making the call to switch from early to late-stage cyclical sectors. In most historical cycles, by the time inflation concerns hit the mainstream, the trade already has been profitable for months, if not quarters. *An upward turn in both the inflation rate and late-to-early cyclical sector performance is a signal that*

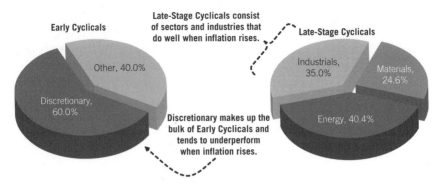

Figure 12.2   Sector Breakdown of Early and Late-Stage Cyclical Groups
Source: Wolfe Trahan & Co.

pressures are building and a portfolio shift is warranted. A straightforward way to gain exposure to this trade is through owning the sector-specific exchange traded funds (ETFs) of the energy, industrials, and materials sectors. Investors who are able to own short positions could buy these sectors as well as sell short the consumer discretionary sector ETF to enhance the trade.

Investors who prefer to own individual stocks within these sectors should focus on identifying companies that are price setters. The concept of pricing power becomes increasingly important for stock pickers as rising inflation turns into a headwind for the market. *The most effective quantitative screen to identify companies that perform well during periods of rising inflation is a combination of market share growth and improving margins.* While not a direct measure of pricing power, this quantitative proxy captures firms that are able to withstand higher inflation by raising prices or improving operating efficiency. Companies that meet these criteria have historically traded with a positive correlation to inflation.

Figure 12.3 shows how companies that screen well for pricing power perform in various inflation environments. When inflation is accelerating strongly, these stocks outperform the broad market by almost four percentage points, and when inflation is falling sharply they underperform by more than six percentage points. The significant performance differential makes this an effective screen on both sides of the inflation trade. An investor could potentially build two portfolios of stocks—one that correlates positively with inflation and the other negatively—and alternate between them as the environment changes.

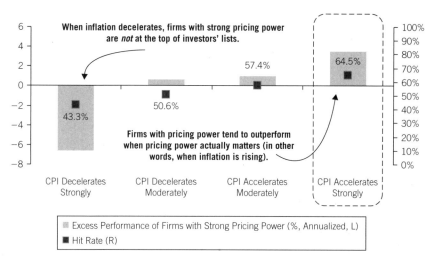

Figure 12.3   Firms with Pricing Power Perform Best as Inflation Rises
Source: Wolfe Trahan & Co.

Bonds typically perform poorly when inflation is increasing as yields rise and prices fall. Normally this happens in conjunction with an accelerating economy, and therefore leading indicators are also rising. Yields ratchet up to compensate for higher inflation, but at the same time they reflect an improvement in growth. It is difficult to accurately separate how much of the increase is attributable to each of these variables. Figure 12.4 shows the relationship between

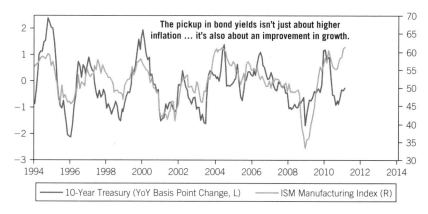

Figure 12.4   Trends in Leading Economic Indicators Typically Help Explain Movements in Bond Yields
Source: Wolfe Trahan & Co.

the yield on the 10-year Treasury bond and the ISM Manufacturing index, a leading indicator. An improving economy is often the signal for investors to sell out of bonds.

When inflation is accelerating due to external pricing pressures, like import and commodity prices, the scenario potentially changes. Figure 12.5 juxtaposes the 10-year Treasury yield with both the ISM Manufacturing Index and the rate of inflation. During the last few years, yields fell alongside inflation, as expected, when leading indicators were declining as well. If leading economic indicators (LEIs) and inflation are in opposition, however, the implication for bonds is unclear. Higher inflation suggests rising bond yields, but a weakening economy and declining LEIs typically imply lower yields

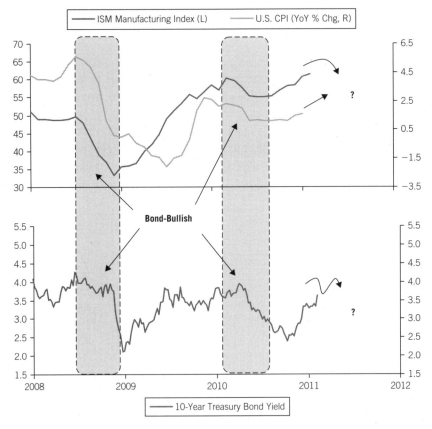

Figure 12.5   Best Time to be Bond-Bullish Is When LEIs and Inflation Are Declining

Source: Wolfe Trahan & Co.

and higher bond prices. The latter is the scenario investors should expect as the environment moves into *Making the Turn*.

Making the Turn—Hedging for Slower Growth

Most investors stop with a surface-level investment philosophy that consists of "stocks go up and bonds go down" during an inflationary period. This is somewhat true in the *Conventional Wisdom* stage of an inflationary period—although sector selection is highly important for owning stocks that benefit during even this first stage. As the inflationary cycle matures, this simple strategy no longer works. When inflationary pressures begin to weigh on leading indicators, as shown in Figure 12.6, investors should become more concerned with preparing their portfolios for slower economic growth than for inflation. Rising prices, especially in food and energy, act like a tax on consumers which can lower future growth prospects.

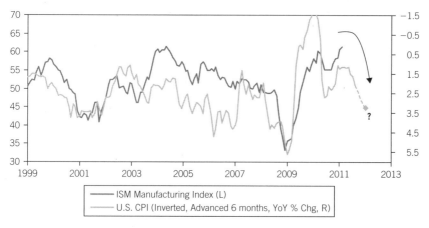

Figure 12.6   Inflationary Pressures Tend to Weigh on Leading Indicators
Source: Wolfe Trahan & Co.

The greatest challenge for investors is how to determine the context of the environment. Often, leading indicators themselves prove the most useful tool for distinguishing between the investment stages of the inflation cycle. The *Prices Paid* components of several regional LEIs are excellent gauges for whether inflation is starting to weigh on growth. The example of the Empire Fed Index is shown in Figure 12.7. Advancing the Prices Paid series forward by six months, and inverting it, gives an indication of where the broader index is headed. Peaks in prices paid generally indicate that inflation will begin choking off growth in the months ahead, and subsequently send LEIs lower.

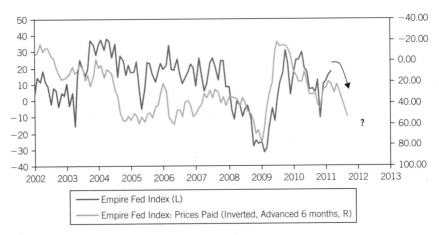

Figure 12.7 Pressure on Leading Indicators from Prices Paid
Source: Wolfe Trahan & Co.

Once leading indicators turn down, the risk-reward profile of the financial markets changes dramatically. Bonds become a preferable investment to equities since yields tend to move lower when economic prospects begin to dim. Stocks tend to experience lower price-to-earnings ratios, companies' profit margins are squeezed, and expected rates of return are lower for equities. Figure 12.8 shows how gross margins for S&P 500 companies usually come under pressure from higher inflation. Pricing power does not matter when consumers are tapped out.

Globalization has significantly impacted the way stocks are exposed to and react to inflation. As the beginning of the world's supply chain, emerging markets have a strong hold on how much American consumers pay for the goods they import. This influence translates directly into the price-to-earnings ratios of domestic stocks. The more the consumer hurts from higher prices, the more likely that companies—and their stock prices—will take a hit. The South Korean KOSPI equity index is an excellent barometer for the tipping point of inflationary pressures and growth. Exports make up more than

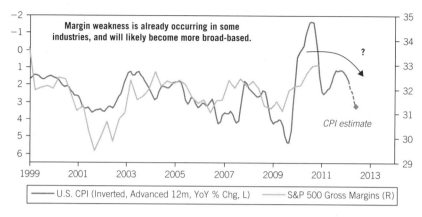

Figure 12.8   Corporate Margins Feel the Pressure of Rising Prices
Source: Wolfe Trahan & Co.

50 percent of South Korean GDP, and therefore, its stock market is highly cyclical. As shown in Figure 12.9, strength in the KOSPI signals that higher prices in raw materials will soon impact stocks in the United States.

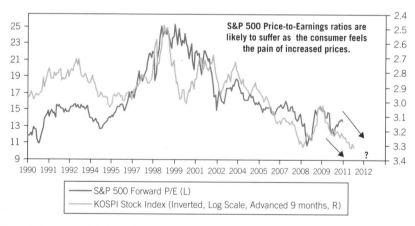

Figure 12.9   Strength in Emerging Markets Eventually Becomes a Headwind for Stocks in the United States
Source: Wolfe Trahan & Co.

Sector leadership rotates again in the *Making the Turn* stage. Stability over cyclicality becomes the preferred sector positioning, and counter-cyclical, or defensive, sectors take over leadership.

The relative underperformance of hyper cyclicals to counter cyclicals—sectors at opposite extremes—is a sign that leading indicators are set to decline. The chart in Figure 12.10 exhibits the tight correlations between these two series.

When *Making the Turn*, the trade shifts in favor of companies with more stable macroeconomic sensitivities. The hyper-cyclical technology sector has the highest correlation with leading indicators, and is essentially allergic to declining growth prospects. The set of charts in Figure 12.11 highlights how the stability of the health

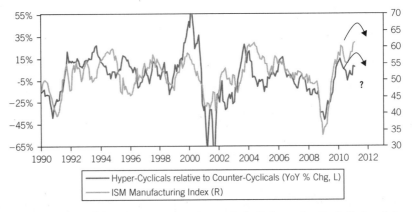

Figure 12.10   Making the Turn: Hyper-Cyclical Sectors Typically Lag as Leading Indicators Fall
Source: Wolfe Trahan & Co.

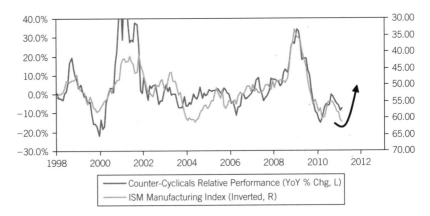

Figure 12.11   Counter-Cyclical Sectors Outperform When LEIs Decline
Source: Wolfe Trahan & Co.

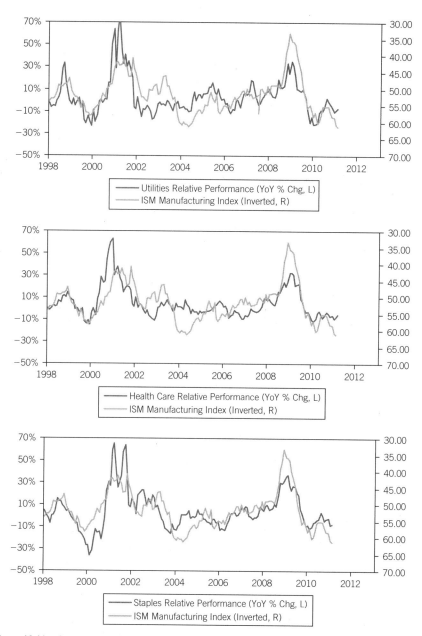

Figure 12.11   Continued

care, utilities, and consumer staples sectors all stand to benefit from a decline in leading indicators.

Policy Responses Bring About Extremes

The Federal Reserve's response to an inflationary period is almost always a policy tightening cycle. The central bank's goal is to raise interest rates and slow growth, but often policy overshoots its target. Excessive corrections have led to a loop of booms and busts as policy has swung back and forth like a Newton's cradle, seen in Figure 12.12. Rarely has the resulting environment become so depressed that a deflationary spiral ensues—a prolonged and severe decrease in general price levels—but there have been several examples of more moderate bouts of deflation from which to draw guidance. The inflation rate has hovered in a fairly benign range during the last several decades, but as recently as 2009 serious deflation was a realistic concern. As the Federal Reserve attempts to direct policy in a globalized world in which it no longer steers the ship, a misalignment of global policy goals could lead to another deflationary period in the near future.

Figure 12.12   Policy Responses Go to Extremes
Source: www.hostdime.com/blog/2010/06/is-your-desk-cool/

Similar to an inflationary environment, deflation's impact on the markets depends on the economic backdrop. Deflation in and of itself is not necessarily bad for markets, but a deflationary *spiral* is another story. Economists and policy makers have typically regarded any specter of deflation as a problem because of its potential to devolve into a deflationary price spiral, conjuring fears of the Great Depression. Modern economic history is littered with examples of the Federal Reserve fighting the devil of inflation, but Chairman Bernanke—who wrote extensively on the Great Depression prior to his central bank tenure—is well aware that run-away deflation can also be an undesirable situation for the economy. Mr. Bernanke indicated in 2002, when he was a Fed Governor, that the United States would implement any policy options necessary to combat deflation. Given his past statements, and his actual policy response to the credit crisis, there is little doubt that even a whiff of deflation would prompt aggressive action.

> I am confident that the Fed would take whatever means necessary to prevent significant deflation in the United States and, moreover, that the U.S. central bank, in cooperation with other parts of the government as needed, has sufficient policy instruments to ensure that any deflation that might occur would be both mild and brief
>
> . . . the U.S. government has a technology, called a printing press (or, today, its electronic equivalent), that allows it to produce as many U.S. dollars as it wishes at essentially no cost. By increasing the number of U.S. dollars in circulation, or even by credibly threatening to do so, the U.S. government can also reduce the value of a dollar in terms of goods and services, which is equivalent to raising the prices in dollars of those goods and services. We conclude that, under a paper-money system, a determined government can always generate higher spending and hence positive inflation.
>
> *Remarks by Governor Ben S. Bernanke before the National Economists Club, Washington, D.C., November 21, 2002, Deflation: Making Sure "It" Doesn't Happen Here*

Disinflation versus Deflation

Recent historical periods of declining inflation, or disinflation, have been supportive for stock market multiples. All else equal, less-rapidly rising prices contribute to better operating margins for companies along two avenues: An increase in the present value of future profits via a lower discount rate, and a decrease in interest paid on debt via lower bond yields. If a *dis*inflationary period extends into a *de*flationary period, however, equity market performance can deteriorate rapidly. Even the fear of a deflationary spiral could impact stock performance, and so it is critical to understand the context in which the inflationary environment is changing.

Periods when the *trend* in inflation is lower but inflation itself is still positive, especially the fairly steady decline from 1980 to 2000, have been good for equities. In contrast, during a deflationary spiral, the downward trend of prices becomes damaging. In other words, when investors fear a deflationary spiral, lower prices send equities lower, but an *improvement* in price trends within a deflationary period helps stocks and multiples recover. One of the telltale signs of the market backdrop, and whether investors fear a deflationary spiral, is the correlation between market performance and inflation trends. This sentiment is also reflected in leading indicator performance. Take the examples of 1990 to 1991 and 2000 through 2002 when inflation rates declined significantly. During both periods leading indicators rose as inflation fell, signaling an optimistic view of lower prices. *If a rebound in LEIs does not occur when inflation falls, the risk of a deflationary spiral is higher.*

The best example in the United States of the changing relationship between inflation trends and equities was the period in and around the Great Depression. Figure 12.13 shows the correlation between the performance of the S&P 500 index and the annual inflation rate from the early 1920s through the late 1940s. In 1922 and 1923, the equity market was rising despite prices deflating because the *rate* of deflation was improving. Stock market performance shows that

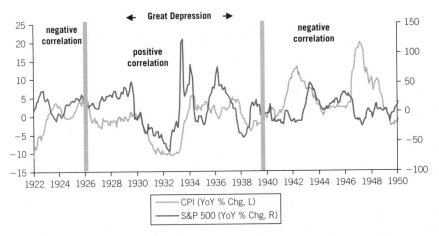

Figure 12.13   Deflationary Spirals Typically Change Correlation Between Inflation and the Equity Market

Source: Wolfe Trahan & Co.

investors were not fearful of worsening deflation. When the rate of change in prices turned positive again, lower rates of inflation generally coincided with positive equity performance. Economic conditions worsened as the years of the Great Depression approached, and equities and prices began moving in tandem. The deeper the deflation spiral went, the lower the S&P 500 index fell. The equity market clearly anticipated a recovery in prices in 1933, and rallied before the official rate of inflation began to improve. As the Depression eased the correlation turned negative again and held during the post-Depression years of the 1940s.

Another notable market metric of deflation is the correlation between inflation and forward price-to-earnings multiples in the consumer discretionary sector. This sector should be a bellwether for inflation pressures, or lack thereof, since consumers are so highly influenced by price changes. Lower prices on staples like food and energy provide more room for discretionary consumption, and should be positive for consumer discretionary stocks. If an improving inflation outlook fails to lift multiples for this sector, it could be an indication that deflation risks are present. A severe divergence could even be an early sign of a deflationary spiral. This is a highly important indicator to watch when the pricing environment is unclear.

It is irrelevant whether the economy experiences only disinflation or outright deflation when it comes to sector positioning; only the direction of the trend matters. The negative correlation between early cyclical sectors and inflation holds when prices are falling as well as rising. In general, a downward movement in inflation is good for consumer-related areas and helps early cyclicals outperform, as shown in Figure 12.14. This pattern held up well during two deflationary periods in the 1940s and 1950s, and also in 2009 when prices tumbled in the recession.

The positive correlation between late-stage cyclicals and prices also holds during deflation, as seen in Figure 12.15. When prices are falling, sectors like energy and industrials tend to perform poorly.

Mild Deflation versus Deflationary Spiral

Historical episodes of deflation can be broadly categorized into two distinct types: *Mild Deflation* and *Deflationary Spiral*. The first, more benign type of deflation tends to be short-lived, and is typically marked by a deceleration in commodity prices and wage growth,

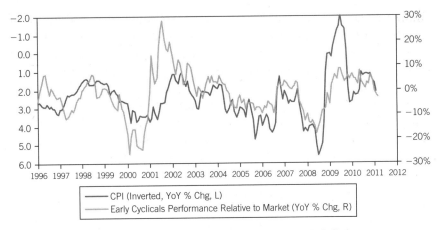

Figure 12.14   Early Cyclicals Typically Outperform the Broader Index in Deflationary Environments
Source: Wolfe Trahan & Co.

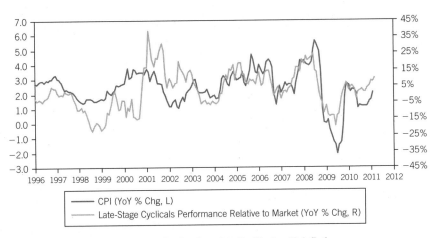

Figure 12.15   Late-Stage Cyclicals Tend to Correlate Positively with Inflation
Source: Wolfe Trahan & Co.

although some other prices may fall as well. In general, these mild bouts have a minimal impact on both the economy and equities, and play out with little long-term damage. The second, more troublesome kind of deflation tends to result in a downward price spiral. These episodes usually last longer and are greater in magnitude than the mild variety, and can ultimately have devastating effects on the economy. The Great Depression is the most notable example of a deflationary spiral in the United States. Table 12.1 details several historical episodes of deflation, both mild and severe.

A bout of even minor deflation can prompt very different reactions from the equity market depending on other economic circumstances. Following World War II, the United States experienced two minor episodes of deflation lasting approximately one year each. The S&P 500 index remained fairly resilient in both periods relative to a deflationary spiral, but one period was far stronger than the other. During the first, in 1949 and 1950, the S&P 500 index fell by about 2.4 percent, but in the second from 1954 to 1955 the index actually rose by 33.7 percent. In both cases commodities declined in tandem with inflation trends, but wages

Table 12.1   An Historical Perspective of Deflationary Episodes in the United States

Deflationary Period	Duration in Months	S&P 500 Returns (CAGR^2 %)	S&P 500 Annualized Returns (CAGR^2 %) Heading Into and Out of Deflation*		Mild or Spiral?
Jan. 1921 to Feb. 1923	26	13.1	Peak to Trough	−16.1	Mild
			Trough to Peak	9.8	
Jul. 1926 to May 1929	35	27.5	Peak to Trough	10.3	Mild
			Trough to Peak	34.7	
Jul. 1930 to Oct. 1933	45	−21.0	Peak to Trough	−35.8	Spiral
			Trough to Peak	31.5	
Mar. 1938 to Aug. 1939	18	7.8	Peak to Trough	−13.6	Mild
			Trough to Peak	−15.8	
May 1949 to Jun. 1950	14	22.6	Peak to Trough	−2.4	Mild
			Trough to Peak	25.8	
Sep. 1954 to Aug. 1955	12	34.9	Peak to Trough	33.7	Mild
			Trough to Peak	9.4	
Mar. 2009 to Oct. 2009	8	66.8	Peak to Trough	−23.2	Mild
			Trough to Peak	33.6	
		Average Peak to Trough		−6.7	Mild
		Average Trough to Peak		18.4	

Notes: Peak To Trough = S&P 500 returns from pre-deflation peak to deflation trough In CPI.
Trough To Peak= S&P 500 returns from deflation trough to post-deflation peak In CPI.

Source: Wolfe Trahan & Co.

behaved differently. As shown in Figure 12.16, wages experienced negative growth in the first episode when equities declined, yet in the second episode, wage growth only *slowed* and equities rallied. *These examples show that negative wage growth is a key factor in determining whether a deflationary spiral ensues, and an excellent indicator for the direction of equities during deflation.*

The link between wage growth and deflation is bad news in light of the data coming out of the housing market. Data for new home sales declined to a fresh low in early 2011. Figure 12.17

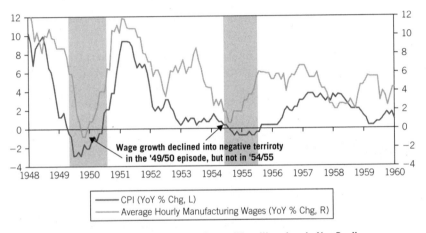

Figure 12.16　Deflationary Episodes Are More Severe When Wage Levels Also Decline
Source: Wolfe Trahan & Co.

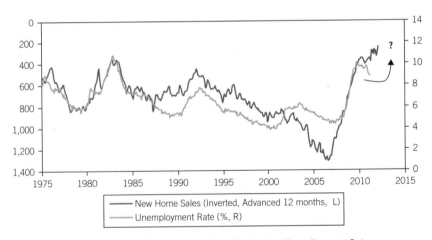

Figure 12.17　Deteriorating Home Sales Not a Good Sign for the Unemployment Rate
Source: Wolfe Trahan & Co.

shows the negative correlation between new home sales (inverted in the chart) and the unemployment rate. If sales data continue to deteriorate, and the employment market follows in line, the United States could proceed directly into a deflationary environment.

Fixed Income Is a Deflationary Safe Haven

The consequences for disinflation and deflation play out across the entire spectrum of the financial markets, not just equities. The best way to hedge a portfolio against a deflationary backdrop is with fixed income instruments. Long-term Treasury bonds were among the top-performing assets in the period leading up to deflation in 2009. Investors sought Treasury securities not only as a safe haven from falling equities, but also as a way to secure an income stream higher than would presumably be available in the future if yields go lower. The predictable relationship between inflation trends and monetary policy contributes to the demand for fixed income. The Fed tends to increase rates to curb inflation and lower rates to stimulate growth. Figure 12.18 illustrates the close relationship between bond yields and inflation trends over the last several decades.

The case for lower bond yields during a deflationary period is reinforced by their relationship with leading indicators. Yields have a strong positive correlation with the ISM Manufacturing Index, as

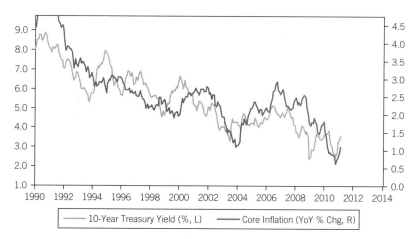

Figure 12.18   Bond Yields Typically Follow Inflation Trends
Source: Wolfe Trahan & Co.

shown in Figure 12.19. When economic prospects deteriorate, leading indicators and bond yields tend to move down in tandem. As investors begin to regain confidence and LEIs bottom, this is a signal that the trend in yields will soon reverse.

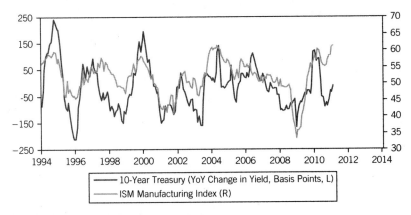

Figure 12.19   Bond Yields and LEIs Move in Tandem
Source: Wolfe Trahan & Co.

The way the shape of the yield curve changes is another means to assess the tradeoff between bonds and stocks. Normally, yields at the short end of the yield curve have the most influence on its shape. A typical flattening of the curve is driven by higher policy rates, which send yields at the short end higher. When deflation is in play, bond yields fall to reflect lower interest rate and growth expectations. In this situation, the yield curve flattens by lowering the longer end. Historically, this is a poor environment for equities but positive for bonds.

The Middle Ground

Extreme inflation trends in either direction tend to disturb the markets. The ideal scenario would be stable growth with low price inflation and an upward trending stock market: Very much what occurred during the 1990s and the early 2000s. The problem for investment managers today is that the Goldilocks "just right" scenario is probably not coming back, at least not for the United States.

The financial industry is a youthful business, especially in the investment management segment, since successful managers tend to accumulate wealth and move on. In a structural sense, the limited experience of financial professionals inhibits collective industry memory and the ability to learn from past bubble episodes. As discussed in Chapter 1, lab-based economic experiments show that market participants recognize past mistakes and change their behavior by the *third* simulated bubble. The reality is that many investment managers do not stick around long enough to experience three bubbles in their careers. Currently, the short tenure of financial professionals means that many managers active today cut their teeth during the Goldilocks era of the 1990s. The experience gained during that time is likely a poor example of what to expect going forward.

The great disinflation that took place during the 1980s led to a period from 1990 through the mid-2000s in which the inflation rate remained between zero and four percent, as shown in Figure 12.20.

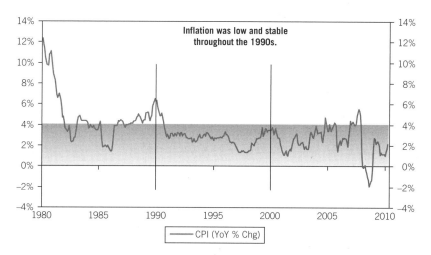

Figure 12.20   Inflation Was "Just Right" During the 1990s
Source: Wolfe Trahan & Co.

Macro trends like globalization, technology, and increasing productivity contributed to the tame environment of the era. Based on more than 100 years of market data, that 0-to-4-percent range for inflation has proven to be the most positive for market multiples, as shown in Figure 12.21. In other words, investors who began their careers in the 1990s have little experience with extremes of inflation or deflation.

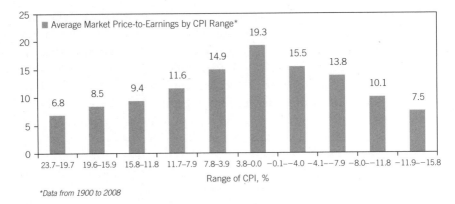

*Data from 1900 to 2008

Figure 12.21   Market Multiples Expand In Low Inflation Environments
Source: Wolfe Trahan & Co.

Goldilocks in the Emerging Markets

Although the Goldilocks economy may prove evasive for the United States in the coming years, if emerging market countries are able to transition to more stable growth and inflation rates their increasing maturity could be very bullish for the global economy. The secular growth story unfolding among the emerging markets makes a strong case for the importance of those countries maintaining better stability over the coming decades.

It appears that China is aware of the need for growth to become more stable. While the Fed is using every tool in its toolbox to speed growth, the government of China claims it will do the opposite in the years ahead. In early 2011, Premier Wen Jiabao said the government has adopted a new five-year plan with an official annual GDP growth target of 7 percent. This is a reduction from the target of 7.5 percent over the past half decade, though in reality growth was closer to 9 percent per year. The aggressive policy tightening that China has already undertaken may have both cyclical and structural goals. Based on the experience of the United States, as shown in Figure 12.21, perhaps bringing inflation closer to the 0-to-4-percent range will be a bullish development for price-to-earnings multiples in China.

Innovations in technology and an increase in trade have resulted in highly synchronized economies. There are obvious benefits to globalization, but the contagion effects felt from the credit crisis and Europe's debt woes have driven investors in search of the ultimate safe haven asset. The dollar has functioned as a refuge in times of distress, but the currency is still vulnerable to Fed policy decisions, and the United States could face its own debt crisis in the years to come. As the correlation of GDP across countries has risen, the price of gold has also increased, as shown in Figure 12.22. Historically, gold has been regarded mostly as a hedge against inflation, but in recent years the metal has continued to rally even when inflation was not on the horizon. It has become an attractive long-term holding for investors who want to hedge the "risk" of globalization.

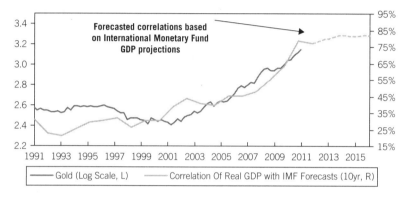

Figure 12.22   A Secular Case for Owning Gold . . . Rising Correlations Equal Rising Risks?
Source: Wolfe Trahan & Co., International Monetary Fund

Chapter Summary

- Some investors would argue that stocks are a big beneficiary of inflation as it can mean greater pricing power for companies, but inflation is a headwind, not a tailwind, to equity market multiples and company margins. A rise in inflation is often followed by a drop in leading indicators.
- Investing appropriately for a higher-inflation environment should be a two-stage event, as summarized in Figure 12.23. The *Conventional Wisdom* period occurs while pricing pressures are building in the economy, and investors should be most concerned about protecting their portfolios from the impact of inflation. During the second stage, *Making the Turn*, consumers already feel the impact of higher prices. Investors should prepare their portfolios for a slowdown in growth.

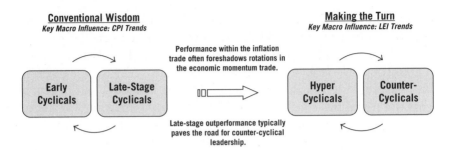

Figure 12.23   Two Stages of Investing for Inflation
Source: Wolfe Trahan & Co.

- Excessive policy corrections have led to a loop of boom and bust periods. Often, the extreme points in inflation over a decade happen within a few years of each other. As the Federal Reserve attempts to direct policy in a globalized world in which it no longer steers the ship, a misalignment of global policy goals could lead to more inflation-turns-to-deflation cycles.
- Deflationary episodes can be broadly categorized into two types: *Mild Deflation* and *Deflationary Spiral*. The first is more benign, tends to be short in duration, and has a minimal impact on the economy and equities. The second usually lasts longer, is greater in magnitude, and tends to have a devastating effect on the economy.
- Historical periods of declining inflation, or disinflation, have been supportive for stock market multiples. If a *dis*inflationary period extends into a *de*flationary period, however, equity market performance can deteriorate rapidly.
- The low inflation and steady growth *Middle Ground* of the 1990s and early 2000s is not coming back in the United States. The global economy would benefit if the emerging markets are able to stabilize their growth and inflation rates at a more sustainable level in the next decade.

PART
V

UNINTENDED CONSEQUENCES AND CREATIVE SOLUTIONS

No one should be fooled by the improvements in gross domestic product and consumer spending experienced through the beginning of 2011. The United States is in a deep hole. The debt-to-GDP ratio stood at more than 97 percent as of March 2011, up from almost 75 percent at the end of 2008 and 57 percent at the end of 2000. The hole is not so deep that temporary fixes couldn't boost growth for a few quarters, but deep enough that meaningful changes must occur to make the improvements last. Let's be honest, nudging interest rates up and down is not going to solve the underlying problems. Structural issues must be addressed with structural, not cyclical, solutions.

Achieving success for any large organization requires a combination of two important factors: thoughtful day to day leadership toward prudent, long-term goals; and a group of competent, motivated people willing to carry out the plan. America has the latter, but is lacking the former. The United States is led by a group of policy makers and politicians who spent their careers creating the fiscal and monetary situations now binding the economy. If the United States government was a public company, it would be kicked out of the S&P 500 index. The country faces the largest structural budget gap in history and the greatest income inequality of the post-war era; meanwhile Americans have witnessed an enormous transfer of wealth from domestic consumers to the Middle East in the form of a lower dollar and higher oil prices. American leaders must look beyond the short-term, easy fixes.

The underlying problems facing the United States are not unique—other nations have tackled them before, most recently Canada during the mid-1990s. The steps taken by Canada's ruling party to reduce historically high deficits and jumpstart growth could serve as a guide for the sacrifices required in the United States. The following figure shows that in less than a decade, the Canadian government balanced its budget and paid down billions of dollars on the national debt primarily through spending cuts and a tailwind of weaker currency and rising exports. The average Canadian reaped the benefits of the austerity measures not long after they were implemented. In 2001, the federal government was able to cut the marginal tax rate for people earning $60,000 to $100,000 Canadian

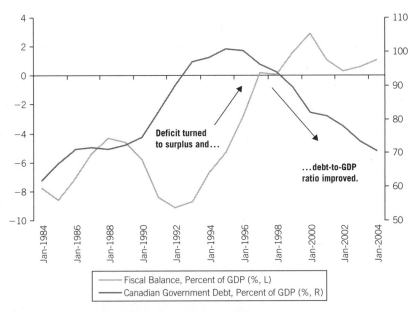

Canada Reduced Record-High Debt and Deficits in the 1990s
Source: Eurostat

dollars per year.[1] The Canadian dollar also strengthened significantly throughout most of the 2000s providing the country's consumers with greater purchasing power in the global marketplace. Canada presented its first balanced budget in more than 30 years in February 1998, three weeks after former President Bill Clinton did the same in the United States. Despite the importance of commodities to Canada's economy, the country was still able to balance its budget in 2008 when commodity prices plunged. There is a blueprint for resolving America's structural problems; the country's leaders just have to follow it.

13

Unintended Consequences

The truth will set you free. But first, it will piss you off.[1]
—Gloria Steinem

Back in 2008, some economists considered the Bernanke-led Federal Reserve the dream team of policy because of the Chairman's extensive studies of the Great Depression. Who better to steer the ship when the United States faced a similar situation? The truth is Chairman Bernanke did a competent job of managing the crisis—if it had been the 1930s! The modern economy is dynamic and globalized to an extent that could not have been imagined during the early twentieth century. Leadership today must consider not only the direct effects of monetary and fiscal policy on the economy, but also the *unintended consequences* of these actions on the social and political fabric of the nation.

QE = WMD?

Warren Buffett called derivatives "financial weapons of mass destruction" (WMD) in the 2002 Berkshire Hathaway annual letter,[2] but he had not yet witnessed the impact of quantitative easing (QE) in the United States. Equating QE with WMDs may sound extreme, but taking a broad view, the comparison is accurate in several ways. The economic implications are clear; quantitative easing causes inflation, and inflation is a drag on growth. It was straightforward to anticipate that QE would depress the dollar, and when the dollar weakens, commodities priced in dollars increase. Even Kansas City Federal Reserve Bank President Thomas Hoenig has publically stated this fact.[3] Ironically, Governor Hoenig raises the link between policy and commodity prices as an example of why the Fed needs to acknowledge improving economic trends and raise interest rates. Instead, he should point to commodity price inflation as the reason that the Fed needs to acknowledge the errors of its past policies and correct them. Dallas Fed Governor Fisher went so far as to imply that inflation may soon seep into core prices: "Having done our job, I see many risks to the Fed overstaying its welcome."[4] He went on to say, "Inflationary impulses are gaining ground in the rest of the world . . . my gut tells me that this will result in some unpleasant general price inflation numbers in the next few reporting periods."[5]

Food Inflation = Hunger in the United States

A drag on GDP growth is not necessarily the most devastating effect of QE, however; the indirect social and political byproducts may prove much greater. These indirect consequences are often ignored because it is very difficult to quantify how much they will ultimately cost. The Fed's stimulative policies were piled onto an already shaky foundation for the average American. Access to credit had propped up consumers' lifestyles for a number of years, but income inequality has been growing in the United States since the 1970s. There are still some people who believe the Reagan-era fallacy of trickle-down economics, but history has proven that there is no such benefit to lower-income earners. An additional 3.7 million people in the United States fell below the poverty line in 2009, propelling the poverty rate to a 15-year high of more than 14 percent, as shown in Figure 13.1. The percentage of children under 18 years old below the poverty line hit almost 21 percent.

Escalating food prices on top of the lingering effects of the recession and deleveraging have only increased the burden on families struggling to make ends meet. In January 2011, almost three million people in New York State were receiving food stamps to help defray the cost of food. Figure 13.2 shows that food stamp recipients in the state jumped 34 percent since January 2009, which was when the commodity price rally began driving up global food prices. One might think, to paraphrase Kanye West, that the Federal Reserve doesn't care about poor people.[6]

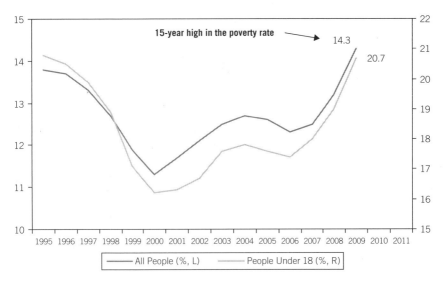

Figure 13.1   Poverty Rate Hit a 15-Year High in 2009
Source: U.S. Bureau of the Census

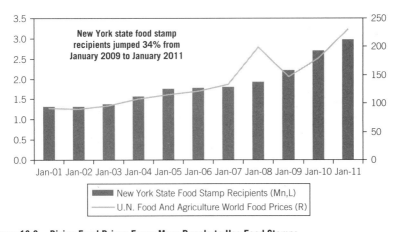

Figure 13.2   Rising Food Prices Force More People to Use Food Stamps
Source: New York State Office of Temporary and Disability Assistance, United Nations

A national hunger survey conducted in February 2011 found that 24 percent of Americans are "very or fairly concerned about being able to afford food at some point in the next year, while 31 percent are slightly worried."[7] Anecdotal evidence of the societal impact of food inflation is apparent across the country. A recent study of hunger at the county level found that hunger exists in

every county and congressional district in the country.[8] A food
bank director in Alabama was quoted by CNN as saying, "If prices
go up any more, you are going to see more people here and other
food banks . . . People that used to give us food are now asking for
it."[9] Survey data from Maryland show that the hunger problem is
spreading beyond urban centers to the suburbs, and into income
brackets well above the official poverty line.[10] A suburban Baltimore
human services center now helps feed people with incomes of
$50,000 to $60,000. The center opened a satellite food bank to keep
up with demand from families and professionals whose incomes
are too far above the poverty guidelines to qualify for federal assistance.[11] The program coordinator at the center said, "We've been
getting folks from the [information technology] industry, folks in
the human services area and the medical field—nursing assistants."
This is not the sign of a society that is doing well.

The drain on income from higher food prices can become
a drag on other areas of the economy the government hopes to
stimulate, like housing. Table 13.1 shows how many of the 37
million Americans served annually by the hunger-relief charity
Feeding America must choose between paying for food and other
necessities.

Although more and more Americans are worse off than they
were a few years ago, conditions are not deteriorating across the
board; the divide between the top earners and everyone else is widening, as shown in Figure 13.3. People with incomes in the highest
quintile have been taking an increasingly larger share of the total
pie, while the share for those at the bottom and in the middle has
declined. From a societal perspective, the implications of widening

Table 13.1   Households Have to Choose Between Paying for Food and Other Essential Services

Percent of Households Having to Choose Between Paying for Food and Other Services	Other Services
46	Utilities or Heating Fuel
39	Rent or Mortgage Payment
34	Medical Bills
35	Transportation

Source: Hunger in America 2010, Feeding America

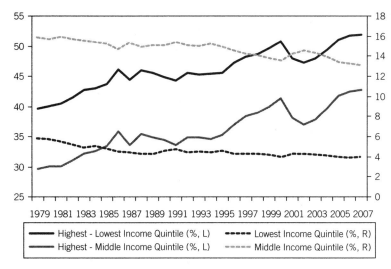

Figure 13.3   Share of Income Rises at the Top but Falls for the Bottom and Middle Segments
Source: Congressional Budget Office, Pre-Tax Income

inequality are even worse than those of poverty alone. The feeling of falling behind encourages people to live beyond their means and hope that their incomes catch up. The world recently witnessed how living on credit to keep up with the Jones' can have an impact well beyond a family's finances.

Inflation and inequality also has played a role in the civil unrest unfolding around the globe. The protests should serve as an example to the United States. The negative psychological impact from struggling to feed one's family contributes to a backdrop of social instability. The surge of Tea Party-type groups that stand for little else than less government is a clear indication of the frustration people feel as a result of stagnant or deteriorating economic quality of life. Growing unrest domestically is not out of the question, particularly with the encouragement of partisan television news personalities fueling the fire.

High Oil Prices Equals Transfer Payment to OPEC

The upheavals in the Middle East and North Africa are the consequences of a perfect storm of economic, social, and political turmoil. The longer-term implications of these nations rising up against authoritarian rulers will not be known for some time, either politically or economically. Even before the protests began, however, oil was on an upward trajectory and generating some unintended political consequences for the United States.

The International Energy Agency (IEA) stated in the *Financial Times* that OPEC will reach $1 trillion in oil export revenues in 2011 if crude oil prices remain above $100 a barrel.[12] Fatih Birol, the Chief Economist of the IEA, said that, "It would be the first time in the history of OPEC that oil revenues have reached a trillion dollars. It's mainly because of higher prices and higher production."[13] Many of OPEC's largest producers are using the elevated revenues to increase public spending, and may become dependent on them. In an effort to stave off the protests spreading through the region, Saudi Arabia passed two financial support packages in early 2011 totaling nearly $130 billion, almost 30 percent of the Kingdom's gross domestic product.[14] In order to meet greater spending needs, Saudi Arabia will require an oil price of $83 per barrel to balance its budget in 2011. Saudi Arabia is essentially creating potential structural problems similar to those of western countries by spending through the "good times". When the next global growth slowdown arrives, the government will not have the money to buy peace and social stability.

> The more they earn, the more they tend to spend. So the oil price they need is ratcheted up.
>
> *Leonidas Drollas, Chief Economist at the*
> *Centre for Global Energy Studies in London,*
> Financial Times, *March 29, 2011*

Russia, the world's top oil producer, saw the cost of its credit-default swaps hit a nearly three-year low as oil passed $111 per barrel in New York and $124 per barrel in Europe in April 2011. The weak dollar has provided a transfer payment from the American consumer to oil-producing nations in the form of higher revenues. According to United Press International, Iran exported more than 844 million barrels of oil in the 12 months from March 2009 to March 2010.[15] The spot price of Europe Brent crude oil nearly doubled from about $46 per barrel on March 31, 2009, to over $80 per barrel on March 31, 2010.[16] At an export rate of 844 million barrels per year, the change in price equates to an additional $29 billion in annual revenues for Iran. It is beyond comprehension that the United States Congress would approve a $29 billion payment to one of the world's most dangerous regimes, but in essence that is exactly what was done by the Federal Reserve. If the Defense Department fully considered the unintended national security consequences of the nation's monetary policy, the Chairman would likely be out of a job.

Chapter Summary

- No one should be fooled by the improvements in GDP and consumer spending experienced through the beginning of 2011. The United States is in a deep hole.
- Structural issues must be addressed with structural, not cyclical, solutions. American leaders must look beyond the short-term, easy fixes.
- The commodity price inflation sparked by the lower dollar has economic, social, and political consequences. The economic implication is lower growth; the social consequences are higher poverty rates and increasing income inequality; and the political results are a transfer of money from the American consumer to oil-producing nations.

CHAPTER 14

Creative Alternatives for the Future

Leadership is, among other things, the ability to inflict pain and get away with it—short-term pain for long-term gain.[1]

—George Will

Big changes come from big ideas. The concept of sweeping reform may seem like wishful thinking in a world run by politicians who get derailed by lobbyists and donors, but sometimes unimaginable things happen in a relatively short period of time. Americans were skeptical when President Kennedy announced his objective in 1961 to go to the moon within the decade, but it was achieved just eight years later. The goals of sustainable monetary policy and fiscal responsibility seem rather tame in comparison, but yet they remain unfulfilled.

There are numerous outside the box reforms that could be game changers for the future of the American economy, but many require an adjustment in perception. Take, for example, the idea of deflation. The word invokes images of the Great Depression for most Americans, and its connotation is decidedly negative. There are some deflationary implications for the consumer, however, that would be positive for the current economic situation in the United States. Deflation has not been good for the Japanese government, but the Japanese consumer has fared considerably better. Inflation erodes the purchasing power of money, but alternatively deflation increases purchasing power in a fashion similar to a tax cut. The math is simple—if consumers are paying less to fill the gas tank they will have more money to spend on discretionary items like iPads and televisions. Deflation also discourages saving since interest rates are effectively negative. A brief and controlled disincentive to save combined with greater purchasing power could provide a catalyst to boost Americans out of their economic malaise. Embracing controversial concepts like this could prove the difference between stagnation and a new period of American growth.

The War on the Deficit

The phrases "war on drugs" and "war on terror" have become part of popular culture in this country, but one more "war" needs to enter the vernacular: The war on the deficit. This is not a partisan war—whether on the left or right side of the political spectrum, neither party can achieve its long-term objectives without a balanced budget. The United States must figure out a way to offset a bloated balance sheet and normalize interest rates while the consumer is deleveraging and consumption is weak. The country is *supposed* to balance its budget when the economy is performing well and policy is not overextended, but this has not happened. This leaves the United States with no bullets left in the chamber, and no margin of error for an unforeseen problem. This is exactly the situation Japan was in when the tragic earthquake and ensuing tsunami struck—large budget deficits and little comfort zone to generate revenue through higher taxes. If a similar situation occurred in the United States, the options for recovery would be limited.

Correcting this situation will require a solid *structural* employment recovery, but a recovery cannot be engineered by putting any additional stress on the budget. Maintaining an ultra-loose monetary policy does nothing to address the non-cyclical problems in the labor market. Although there are very few solutions that are pro-growth, the best way to achieve these difficult goals is through factors that increase the potential level of GDP. The two factors that have the greatest affect on potential GDP are productivity and population, as shown in Figure 14.1.

Increase Productivity

The United States has one of the highest corporate tax burdens in the world. Countries such as Canada, Sweden, and Denmark,

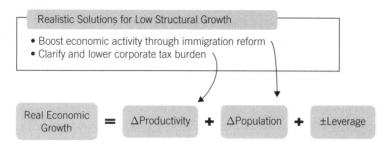

Figure 14.1   Increasing Potential GDP
Source: Wolfe Trahan & Co.

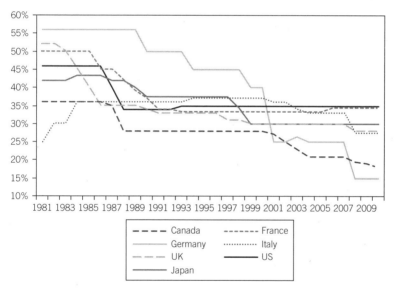

Figure 14.2   The United States Now Has the Highest Corporate Income Tax Rate in the Group of 7
Source: OECD Tax Database, Table II.1

which many Americans regard as tax and spend socialist economies, have lower corporate tax rates than America. Figure 14.2 shows how the United States has fallen behind other major developed economies in terms of competitiveness of corporate tax rates.

High corporate taxes tend to hinder investment and economic activity, but an *uncertain* future tax environment can be just as stunting. Temporary tax breaks give corporations only myopic visibility; in other words, they still do not know what their tax bill is going to look like five years down the road. Permanently lowering the tax rate and simplifying the code could promote higher productivity, and put an end to the uncertainty surrounding the fiscal future for corporations. Companies have cash on the books, but have been unwilling to invest in people or capital in the United States. Multi-national corporations choose to keep their cash overseas where the tax environments are much more favorable. The unintended consequences of an ill-thought-out tax structure are to compensate other countries with the rewards of American companies' innovation and creativity. The temporary Bush-era personal tax cuts extended in late 2010 also did nothing to address underlying growth problems; they were just a surface-level transfer payment instead of an investment in job creation. The amount of money foregone by the United States government in order to extend the cuts could have been used much more efficiently, for example to reduce the payroll taxes paid by businesses.

Politicians should examine the less-obvious effects of tax policy before succumbing to knee-jerk, party-line stances. Balancing the budget actually would have positive, trickle-down effects. Democrats are less likely than Republicans to support lower corporate taxes, but the secondary effects could be highly beneficial to social programs. A balanced budget would generate far less pressure to cut programs associated with education and social welfare. The Republicans should favor a balanced budget so that they could muster support for tax cuts and address longer-term spending issues like entitlement programs. Perhaps Congressional term limits are a solution to this partisan problem. Game theory teaches us that economic players are incentivized to act in the mutual best interest only in the "final period" of a game. If we put more of the country's politicians in their final term at once, there might be a greater probability that they vote in the best interest of their constituents instead of strictly along party lines.

Increase Population

A surface-level analysis may conclude that addressing the government's financial problems is a zero-sum game—moving money around between federal, state, and local governments produces some winners and some losers, but the whole is not better off. Looking

Wolfe Trahan Client Survey

How do you feel about increasing immigration and visas for entrepreneurs and highly educated immigrants: Support or Oppose?

Support or Oppose	Percentage
Support	93.4
Oppose	6.6

Survey conducted March 25, 2011.
Total respondents to this question: 725

deeper, there are ways that the total pie could be increased. Growing the population, and ultimately the tax base, could prove one of the missing puzzle pieces, but population trends are moving in the opposite direction. One of the most significant game changers could be immigration reform.

China's one-child policy has been anticipated to be detrimental to long-term sustainable growth in the country. As the massive population ages, more and more retirees will become dependent on a shrinking pool of working-age people. Poor economic prospects could create the same dynamic in the United States. The birth rate in this country has been falling structurally for several decades, but in the last few years it has moved precipitously lower along with the economic climate. Figure 14.3 illustrates the declining birth rate's affect on total population growth.

There is no doubt that immigration is a controversial issue in the United States. Politicians stoke images of undocumented workers sneaking across the border to steal American jobs, but this is a bait and switch to deflect attention from the very real, structural employment problem. Many illegal immigrants are working jobs that Americans won't perform, like seasonal farm laborers and domestic positions with no benefits—not nabbing a high-paying engineering position out from under a recent college graduate. Many Americans don't understand how the right kind of immigration can be good for growth. The misconceptions surrounding this

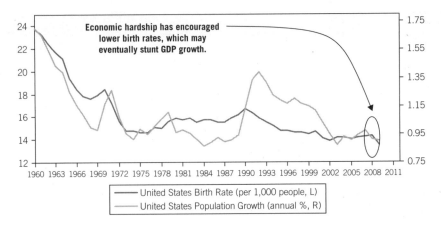

Figure 14.3   Immigration Reform Could Be a Solution for Population Decline
Source: Wolfe Trahan & Co.

issue are rooted in ignorance, but as long as the inflammatory rhetoric remains, xenophobia will hamper economic prosperity. The brand of this country is being tarnished by the Bill O'Reillys and Glenn Becks of the world who want nothing more than to spark controversy for ratings.

This closed-minded attitude is ironic since the history of the United States is rooted in immigration. Americans today glorify the immigrants who arrived in the country's first 200 years as hardworking people looking to make better lives for their families, but they believe current immigrants are coming to live off the system. Of course there are some people trying to make it to America to do just that, but immigration can be reformed in a way that is beneficial to society.

One method of encouraging growth-positive immigration is by offering guaranteed visas for immigrants who have a university degree, no criminal record, and the means to buy a home for cash. This policy could prop up the housing market, help recapitalize banks by reducing borrowing needs, and boost the entrepreneurial segment of the economy. The maturation of emerging markets has created massive wealth in countries like China, India, and Brazil, but currently these dollars are better spent at home. More than one-third of the wealthiest people on the Forbes' Billionaire list in 2011 were citizens of emerging market countries, with a total net worth of more than $1 trillion.[2] Increasing visa availability and facilitating transition to citizenship for immigrants who can meet a set of minimum investment requirements in targeted areas of the economy could attract job-creating entrepreneurs.

The United States should promote its lower violent crime rate as a draw for wealthy families concerned about safety in Central and South America or Africa. According to the National Council of Private Security, spending on private security services in Mexico rose 11 percent between 2009 and 2010, and in Brazil private security is among the fastest growing segments of the economy.[3,4] The relative security of America is a huge selling point to potential immigrants, possibly outweighing taxation issues. Opening our borders to business people looking for a more civil society, and who are willing to invest in the United States economy and create jobs—along with a more favorable corporate tax code—could have a significant impact on potential growth.

The United States should also act to keep students for the long term who are already studying in the country. For several decades, students from around the world came to earn coveted degrees at American universities and then made their best effort to find jobs here. The shift in economic prospects between the United States and emerging economies has changed that dynamic. Now, foreigners are still coming to America to study, but then returning to invest their intellectual capital in their home countries.

According to a 2009 study, most foreign nationals earning degrees at universities in the United States believe that American higher education is the best in the world, but yet do not plan to remain permanently in the United States after graduation.[5] One of the study's co-authors claims that "foreign students have a sense that the United States is closing down as a land of opportunity."[6] She states this is happening even though "the U.S. has long been a magnet for the best and the brightest from around the world, and even though we have benefitted from many of these students—who are the cream of the crop—starting businesses that generate net wealth and expand opportunities for everyone."[7] The report points out that foreign students have gone on to become disproportionately represented in the ranks of America's top entrepreneurs, and cites as examples the co-founders of technology firms such as Google, Intel, eBay, and Yahoo.

The survey commissioned by the Ewing Marion Kaufman Foundation brought to light some alarming views regarding the United States:[8]

- Only seven percent of Chinese students and 25 percent of Indian students surveyed said the best days for the United States economy lie ahead.
- Approximately 74 percent of Chinese students and 86 percent of Indian students said their home countries' economies will grow faster in the future than they have in the past decade.
- Three-quarters of Chinese students and almost 84 percent of Indian students said it would be difficult to find a job in their field in the United States.
- Only 6 percent of Indian students, 10 percent of Chinese students, and 15 percent of European students said they wanted to remain permanently in the United States after graduation.

The United States could stem the brain drain by putting American university graduates on a fast-track to citizenship, subject to thorough background investigations. Opening satellite Immigration and Naturalization Services offices in major universities to guide visa applications could help retain American-educated students. This country currently is shunning an important source of tax revenue and job creation by painting immigration with such a broad brush.

Chapter Summary

- Big changes come from big ideas. There are numerous outside the box reforms that could be game changers for the future of the American economy, but many require an adjustment in perception.
- The war on the deficit should be bipartisan; neither party can achieve its objectives without a balanced budget. Although there are very few solutions that are pro-growth, the best way to achieve these difficult goals is through factors that increase the potential level of GDP.

- Temporary tax breaks give corporations only myopic visibility; in other words, they still do not know what their tax bill is going to look like five years down the road. Permanently lowering the tax rate and simplifying the code could promote higher productivity, and put an end to the uncertainty surrounding the fiscal future for corporations.
- Growing the population, and ultimately the tax base, could prove one of the missing puzzle pieces, but population trends are moving in the opposite direction. One of the most significant game changers could be immigration reform.

Epilogue: The Financial Services Industry in the Era of Uncertainty

The future is always uncertain, but the circumstances the United States finds itself in today make the path ahead for policy even more unclear. Normalizing monetary policy in the short run and addressing the country's fiscal shortfalls in the longer-run are dilemmas that weigh on the future of the financial markets as well. The path that appears most likely—inflation followed by disinflation or deflation—implies that the equity markets have a rocky road ahead. An industry levered to a rising equity market will have to adapt to an environment in which market conditions are more unpredictable, and not always supportive.

The decade of the 2000s was a rude awakening for both professional and amateur investors. Assumptions that equities always won in the long run were tested and failed. From January 1, 2000, through December 31, 2009, the S&P 500 index returned less than −9.0 percent.[1] Over the same period, the Lehman (now Barclays) Aggregate Bond Index was up almost 85 percent and Gold gained 280 percent.[2] Asset allocation models all over Wall Street were turned upside down. Despite the nervousness the latest recession caused, many financial professionals still expect a return to the good old days of double-digit equity returns and supportive policy. The reappearance of these Goldilocks conditions is unlikely. Going forward, a macro perspective will be the key to determining the appropriate asset allocation, sector allocation, and stock selection.

Scandals have marred hedge funds in recent years, but an unstable U.S. equity market may prove supportive of the industry. Demand for long-short funds that are able to produce positive returns in differing market conditions should be strong during times of uncertainty. Macro funds that invest across asset classes and can profit from global themes will be among the beneficiaries of equity market turmoil. In the long-only investment management world, anemic returns should increase investors' appetites for dividends and income-producing funds.

The image of the financial industry was dealt a major blow during the credit crisis and ensuing recession, as the veil was lifted for public viewing of the corruption and greed on Wall Street. The industry either turned a blind eye to the underlying problems in the mortgage market or just did not see them, but neither choice inspires confidence. Wall Street strategists and seemingly independent academic economists were in bed with governments, and profited enormously from producing publications that supported their policies. Only as the dust cleared did the public realize how much of the research was for hire. Despite public outrage and some acrimonious Congressional hearings, there were few meaningful changes, and the industry has largely returned to business as usual. Only time will tell how the industry in general will adapt to the tumultuous times ahead, but without a doubt, macro trends will play a significant role in investing successfully.

Notes

Part 1

1. Wolfe Trahan Client Survey conducted March 25, 2011.

Chapter 1

1. www.quotedb.com/quotes/3038.
2. Universe = S&P 100.
3. "Bubbles, Crashes, and Endogenous Expectations in Experimental Spot Asset Markets," *Econometrica*, 56 (1988), pp. 1119–1151.

Chapter 2

1. http://thinkexist.com/quotation/globalization_is_a_fact_of_life-but_i_believe_we/151761.html
2. "Geithner Sees Europe Managing Crisis Without Fallout for U.S. Economy," Ian Katz and Rich Miller, Bloomberg News, May 15, 2010.
3. "The Economic Outlook and Monetary Policy," Chairman Ben S. Bernanke, at the Federal Reserve Bank of Kansas City Economic Symposium, Jackson Hole, Wyoming, August 27, 2010.

Chapter 3

1. http://thinkexist.com/quotation/we_have_for_the_first_time_an_economy_based_on_a/324469.html
2. As diversified financials have overtaken Banks as the financial sector's largest industry, the macro forces that influence the sector have also changed. Due to diversified financials making up 50 percent of the sector's weighting, financials now trade like a classic cyclical sector.

Chapter 4

1. http://thinkexist.com/quotation/markets_are_constantly_ in_a_state_of_uncertainty/207869.html

Chapter 5

1. www.brainyquote.com/quotes/keywords/denial_2.html# ixzz1IuOv3E7A
2. "Drop Foreseen in Median Price of Homes in U.S." by David Leonhardt and Vikas Bajaj, *New York Times*, August 26, 2007.
3. Testimony before the Joint Economic Committee, United States Congress, *The economic outlook*, Chairman Ben S. Bernanke, March 28, 2007.
4. "Fed 'not currently' predicting US recession: Bernanke," AFP, January 10, 2008.
5. Alternative A-paper is a mortgage considered riskier than a prime mortgage due to the borrower's credit rating, lack of income documentation, or high loan values. It is assumed to be less risky than a subprime mortgage.
6. Includes GNMA, FNMA, and FHLMC mortgage-backed securities and CMOs, CMBS, and private-label MBS/CMOs.
7. United States Securities and Exchange Commission Press Release, "SEC Charges Two Former Bear Stearns Hedge Fund Managers With Fraud," June 19, 2008.
8. Financial Crisis Inquiry Commission Preliminary Staff Report, "Governmental Rescues of 'Too-big-to-fail' Financial Institutions," August 31, 2010.

Chapter 6

1. http://thinkexist.com/quotation/it_ain-t_what_you_don-t_ know_that_gets_you_into/215214.html
2. "Why politics and investing don't mix," Barry Ritholtz, *Washington Post*, February 6, 2011.
3. Transcript, *The Fog of War: Eleven Lessons from the Life of Robert S. McNamara*, www.errolmorris.com/film/fow_transcript.html
4. www.quotationspage.com/quote/38206.html
5. www.condoflip.com, now redicted to www.zilbert.com
6. Edward Chancellor, *Devil Take the Hindmost*, New York: Plume, 2000, pp. 191–199.

7. John M. Berry, "Home Prices Won't Directly Affect Fed Rates," Bloomberg News, April 7, 2005.

8. National Bureau of Economic Research Business Cycle Dating Committee, United States Business Cycle Expansions and Contractions, www.nber.org/cycles/cyclesmain.html.

Chapter 7

1. Henry Hazlitt. *Economics in One Lesson*. New York: Three Rivers Press, 1946.

2. Economic New Release, *Employment Situation Summary*, Bureau of Labor Statistics, May 6, 2011.

Chapter 8

1. http://quotationsbook.com/quote/22815/#axzz1IuQkKQiX

2. *The Federal Reserve System: Purposes and Functions*, ninth edition, June 2005, Publications Committee, Board of Governors of the Federal Reserve System, Washington, D.C.

3. "The Fed's dual mandate dates to a 1946 act," Ken McLean, Letters to the Editor, November 25, 2010.

4. The NBER Business Cycle dating committee defined the recession as beginning in December 2007 and ending in June 2009.

5. The Taylor Rule was developed by the economist John Taylor. According to this policy rule the federal funds rate is increased or decreased according to what is happening to both real GDP and inflation. In particular, if real GDP rises one percent above potential GDP the federal funds rate should be raised, relative to the current inflation rate, by .5 percent. And if inflation rises by one percent above its target of 2 percent, then the federal funds rate should be raised by .5 percent relative to the inflation rate. When real GDP is equal to potential GDP and inflation is equal to its target of 2 percent, then the federal funds rate should remain at about 4 percent, which would imply a real interest rate of 2 percent on average. (The Taylor Rule, Homer Jones Memorial Lecture Series, Federal Reserve Bank of St. Louis.)

6. "Report on Foreign Portfolio Holdings of U.S. Securities," Department of the Treasury, Federal Reserve Bank of New York,

Board of Governors of the Federal Reserve System, April 2011. Data as of June 2010, 53.0 percent.

7. *CIA World Factbook*, online version, Japan Public Debt as Percent of GDP, https://www.cia.gov/library/publications/the-world-factbook/rankorder/2186rank.html?countryName=Japan&countryCode=ja&regionCode=eas&rank=2#ja

Chapter 9

1. www.brainyquote.com/quotes/quotes/j/johnmaynar101942.html
2. "Household Income for States: 2008 and 2009," Census Bureau, September 2010. Data as of 2009.
3. "Fact Sheet on the Framework Agreement on Middle Class Tax Cuts and Unemployment Insurance," Office of the Press Secretary, The White House, December 7, 2010.
4. USA Today/Gallup poll conducted September 13–16, 2010.
5. "Four pinocchios for the American public on the budget," Glenn Kessler, *Washington Post*, March 3, 2001.
6. Ibid.
7. Program for Public Consultation (PPC) is affiliated with the School of Public Policy at the University of Maryland. The study was fielded by Knowledge Networks. "How the American Public Would Deal with the Budget Deficit: A Study by the Program for Public Consultation and Knowledge Networks," by Steve Kull, Clay Ramsay, Evan Lewis, and Stefan Subias, February 3, 2011.
8. "It's the Inequality, Stupid," by Dave Gilson and Carolyn Perot, *MotherJones*, March/April 2011 issue.
9. The tax rate is inverted in the chart so the higher the line, the lower the tax rate.
10. "California Town Thrives by Outsourcing All Its Jobs," by Dan Weil, moneynews.com, July 28, 2010.
11. "Roads to Ruin: Towns Rip Up the Pavement," by Lauren Etter, *Wall Street Journal*, July 17, 2010.
12. "How the American Public Would Deal with the Budget Deficit: A Study by the Program for Public Consultation and Knowledge Networks," by Steve Kull, Clay Ramsay, Evan Lewis, and Stefan Subias, February 3, 2011.

Chapter 10

1. www.brainyquote.com/quotes/keywords/short-term.html
2. "It's the Inequality, Stupid," by Dave Gilson and Carolyn Perot, *MotherJones,* March/April 2011 issue.
3. Reference some income studies.

Chapter 11

1. http://thinkexist.com/quotation/inflation_is_taxation_without/ 175771.html
2. "Food Price Hike Drives 44 Million People into Poverty," Press Release No:2011/333/PREM, The World Bank, February 15, 2011.

Chapter 12

1. www.great-quotes.com/quote/525236
2. Percent Compound Annual Growth Rate
3. Percent Compound Annual Growth Rate

Part 5

1. Personal income tax rates and thresholds for central governments (Table I.1), OECD Tax Database.

Chapter 13

1. http://thinkexist.com/quotation/the_truth_will_set_you_ free-but_first-it_will/207998.html
2. Berkshire Hathaway Inc., 2002 Annual Report, Warren Buffett, February 21, 2003.
3. "Hoenig Says Fed Shares Blame for Higher Commodity Prices; Urges Tightening," Vivien Lou Chen, Bloomberg News, March 30, 2011.
4. Federal Reserve Bank of Dallas President Richard Fisher, Society of American Business Editors and Writers 2011 Annual Conference, April 8, 2011.
5. Ibid.
6. "Kanye West's Torrent of Criticism, Live on NBC," Lisa de Moraes, *Washington Post,* September 3, 2005.

7. Survey conducted by Hart Research Associates, commissioned by the Food Research and Action Center (FRAC) and Tyson Foods.
8. "Hunger in America 2010 National Report Prepared for Feeding America," Mathematica Policy Research Inc., Final Report, January 2010.
9. Community Market director Elsie Lott, "Rising food prices could drive up rates of hunger," by John Sepulvado, CNN Radio, March 16, 2011.
10. "Hunger in America 2010 National Report Prepared for Feeding America."
11. Quinton Askew, program coordinator at the North Laurel-Savage Multiservice Center, Columbia, Maryland. "Hunger Issues Said to Be Striking Maryland Suburbs," by Lisa Rossi, Essex-Middle River Patch, April 4, 2011.
12. "OPEC set for $1,000bn in export revenues," Sylvia Pfeifer, Javier Blas, and David Blair, *Financial Times*, March 29 2011.
13. Ibid.
14. "Saudi Arabia Keeps Wary Eye on Domestic Inflation," by Yousef Gamal El-Din, CNBC.com, April 6, 2011.
15. "Iran oil exports top 844 million barrels," UPI.com, June 17, 2010.
16. U.S. Energy Information Administration.

Chapter 14

1. www.brainyquote.com/quotes/quotes/g/georgewill166519.html
2. "The World's Billionaires," www.forbes.com/wealth/billionaires, March 9, 2011.
3. "Mexico drugs war—as violence spirals, so does spending on security," Reuters, Guardian.co.uk, October 13, 2010.
4. "Democracy and Citizen Security," Political Database of the Americas, Federative Republic of Brazil, September 15, 2007.
5. "Losing the World's Best and Brightest," Vivek Wadhwa, AnnaLee Saxenian, Richard Freeman, and Alex Salkever, commissioned by the Ewing Marion Kauffman Foundation, March 2009.
6. "U.S. economy spurs foreign students to return home, study says," Kathleen Maclay, Press Release, UC Berkeley News, March 19, 2009.

7. Ibid.

8. "Losing the World's Best and Brightest."

Epilogue

1. Standard & Poor's.

2. Barclays Capital Indices, London Bullion Market Association.

About the Authors

François Trahan is Vice Chairman and Chief Investment Strategist of Wolfe Trahan & Co., a premier investment research boutique. An economist by training with a master's degree in econometrics, he is widely praised for his differentiated insights into the drivers and dynamics of the market place and his unique understanding of the business cycle. *Institutional Investor* magazine ranked Mr. Trahan top portfolio strategist for the past three years and in five of the past six years. In 2010, he also ranked second in the quantitative research category. Prior to joining Wolfe Trahan, he was Executive Managing Director and Chief Investment Strategist at International Strategy and Investment Group (ISI), as well as head of ISI's Quantitative Research Team. Mr. Trahan was formerly with Bear Stearns & Co. where he served as a Senior Managing Director and Chief Investment Strategist. Earlier, he worked for Ned Davis Research and the Bank Credit Analyst Research Group. Mr. Trahan received his Bachelor's and Master's degrees in economics and econometrics from the University of Montreal.

Katherine Krantz is a Founding Partner and Chief Economic Strategist of Miracle Mile Advisors, LLC, an independent registered investment advisory firm that manages money for high-net-worth families. Her background as both an econometrician and economist enables her to lead the asset allocation and quantitative analysis efforts of the firm, which specializes in global macro allocation strategies primarily populated with exchange-traded funds. Ms. Krantz was previously in the Private Wealth Management Division of Morgan Stanley, & Co., and the fund of funds division of AXA Investment Managers. Earlier in her career she worked for Ned Davis Research and the Bank Credit Analyst Research Group. Ms. Krantz received her Bachelor's degree in economics and mathematical methods in the social sciences from Northwestern University, and her Master's in economics and econometrics from McGill University, where she was also a lecturer in economics, statistics, and econometrics.

About the Digital Companion

The companion web site offers readers the ability to input their own current assumptions for inflation and growth and receive a set of macro-driven investment recommendations for each combination.

Please visit www.wiley.com/go/uncertainty and enter "global" to gain access to this interactive model.

Index